To my friend
Ester

Love Always

[signature]

10/14/2011

From Me To YOU

Outskirts Press, Inc.
Denver, Colorado

Product of My Environment
All Rights Reserved.
Copyright © 2010 From Me to You
v3.0

Outskirts Press, Inc.
http://www.outskirtspress.com

ISBN: 978-1-4327-5592-8

Outskirts Press and the "OP" logo are trademarks belonging to Outskirts Press, Inc.

PRINTED IN THE UNITED STATES OF AMERICA

Foreword & Acknowledgements

- Meechie gave the title, family did the editing

As I was looking back at my life, and talking to my family of the positive and negative my nephew Demetrius Craig mentioned that I was a "Product Of My Environment". Wow that sounded so right.

My brothers George Jr., Craig, Raif and my sister, Vanessa, helped edit the book. And helped me open my soul and deal with the pain of placing my life on paper.

Contents

CHAPTER 1

Black and Bald

I lived at 888 Greene Avenue, in Bed Stuy, Brooklyn. We lived on the third floor. A three bedroom apartment with a long hallway. There was no elevator so you had to walk all the way up. There was my father, an ex Air force man who loved to cook. He was very handsome with his dark complexion and boyish country look. My father was born and raised in Baton Rouge, LA. He seemed like he never aged a day in his life. He smoked a pipe cherry blend tobacco. He was 5'11, with a slender build. Then there was my mother. Sunny brown complexion. Straight out of Harlem. With attitude to spare. She wore these cat glasses that hung on her nose when she got angry. A very outspoken women in every way. I also had three brothers George Jr., Craig, and Raif.

What a day, this was the day all black people where saying it loud "I'm Black and I'm Proud". As I looked in the mirror in our little bathroom all I would see is my dark skin, big eyes and bald head. What is there to be proud of, I thought to myself. I was getting dressed and my brothers wanted to come in. "No you guys stay out I'll be out in a minute." Then the door opened up and there she was. My mother. My mother was the boss of the house, and she hated me. Ever since I could remember she hated me.

I don't know why but she said that she hated me from the day I was born. Anyway. She grabs me and pulled me out of the bathroom. I cried. And my brothers laughed. I looked down and there I was standing there naked. I ran to my bedroom and got dressed. That's how I started most of my mornings. Crying. I was bald headed because my mother burned off my hair with a hot comb. Why? I don't know. So I went to school like that most mornings pushing back the pain of the morning.

At school I felt so alone. No one liked me there. Man my mother didn't like me and the kids in my school didn't like me. I was tall and skinny. I had bald nappy short hair and I couldn't do anything right. I wasn't smart and it showed. To make matters worse I was real dark skin. Like African skin dark. No boys wanted to go with me. They called me bald headed and blackie. I had to sit through school all day looking at the clock on the wall wondering when will 3:00 come. My teachers used to try to talk to me. It was like they seen me sad and they used to ask me how I got that black eye? I wouldn't tell them my mother did it. I just didn't say anything. I could see in their eyes that they wanted to say something to me but before they could the bell would ring and I would pack up and run out. As I walked out side I notice a lot of people on the steps. I looked and they where surrounding someone. Then through the crowd I saw him. It was my brother, my brother George. He was two years younger then me. My brother was smart and he wasn't as dark as me he had my mothers complexion. Everyone always said how smart he was. I ran over and said what's going on?

One of the boys said, "Your brother is really smart he knows how to spell education." Do you know how to spell it he asked me? I said yes EDUCATION. My brother said no it's EDUCUTION. And everyone started to laugh as we walked home through the park that we always walked through. My brother always made me fell good by not bringing embarrassing situations up. It was like he knew that I didn't want to talk about it. So we walked in silence. I met up with the only person that liked me Baby Doll. I was glad to see her I said, "my brother knows how to spell education" she said, "he does, wow he's smart." What are you doing today? Nothing got to do my homework and maybe I could come outside. See you later ok. Yeah see you later. We walked up three flights of stairs and opened the door. I usually made sure my mother was not standing behind the door waiting to hit me, but I was so happy about my brother knowing how to spell education I forgot. WHAM! I felt this pain. I lost focus for a while then WHAM! Again then I got my balance and focus. That's when I saw her standing there with a broom hitting me. My chest hurt and then the second blow landed on my arm. I stop asking why and just took it. The broom handle broke and I was hoping that she wouldn't keep hitting me like the last time and she didn't. It was ok, the pain was over after she would stop hitting me. I learned to turn the pain from one place to another. I would go inside of myself to where the pain was and sweep it to the tips of my fingers and it was gone.

My father was a working man. And I looked just like him I mean I really look like him. Everyone said it. I believe it was true. But he was gone a lot working so that we would have food on the table. My father was the oldest of eight. He met my mother when he was home from the service one day. He was a cook in the Air Force. They fell in love and I was born but he didn't marry her until he came back a year later. So I was born a bastard. Everyone said when he seen me in the hospital that he couldn't deny me. I loved him, he used to tell my mother not to hit me like that. But then they would get into a fight. And my mother would always win. Because dad would just leave or just stop talking. Then mom got slick she started hitting me early and not in the face no more. So by the time he came home all the beatings stop and we looked like nothing was wrong. **Anyway.**

Later that night when he came home he learned that his first-born son was very smart and that his first born was not. I had to read a story and answer the question in my history book. But the word "concerned" was hard I keep saying concert. He got mad and the madder he got the louder he got. His eyebrows would crest in the middle of his face and a vein would pop out of his neck and then the finger would come out. The more he pointed to me and yelled "concerned" I said concert. Then my brother George came and said sis concerned not concert. There is no T in concerned. My father said, yeah stupid no T. I didn't mine that he called me stupid I loved him and he never hit me so anyway I was called worse by my mother. Then Craig, my middle brother, and Raif, my youngest brother, said yeah stupid no T. This instantly became a song. Yeah stupid no T. Yeah stupid no T. My brothers use to tease me all the time. I think in their own way they know that mom didn't like me so they jump on the band wagon. The more they sang the more tears ran down my cheeks till my father just gave up on me and walked away. He did that a lot gave up on me and walked away. At least he didn't beat me. I'm telling you with his big hands I'm really glad.

The next day I woke up and went to the bathroom fully dressed and looked in the mirror and saw the same thing a black bald headed girl. I thought why am I here no one wanted me. God hates me.

After school my mother let me go outside. She said she was tired of looking at me. That was ok with me because I was tired of looking at her too. She didn't have to tell me twice I ran down stairs and went to the park which was across the street from my building. The park had one swing in it and it was broken. It had a sliding board and no one would go on it because well you just didn't. So all kids had to play with was bums. Me and Baby Doll went looking for a drunk on a bench. I said there's one. See we lived in that type of neighborhood where there was always a drunk man on the bench of the school yard. Oh yeah I didn't tell you the park was our school yard. We use to wake him up and he use to chase us all over the place. That was fun. We called that game running from the drunken guy. There was also Bruce the drug addict that used to get high and naked and when he did that the singing out of his window would start. Now he was fun. He used to steal things and give it to the kids on the block. One day he came around with a whole box of watches and potato chips and just gave it to us. Everyone had a watch and potato chips that day. In return for him being so nice to us when he had his friend doing heroin outside our door we didn't bother him. I didn't like the smell of heroin. I remember one day Pete said to me, "never use this stuff ok". I thought to myself yeah ok. I didn't like the way burnt feet smelled anyway. Don't forget the women would wait for the men to get paid on the corner. They were the worse of all the Hoes. "Street Walkers" ladies of the night. I hated them, and I didn't know why, I just did.

Anyway.

Well anyway Baby Dolls brothers were bad I mean bad she had this one brother named David who seems to be mad all day long. I don't think I've ever seen him smile. He would be with all these mad boys too who never smiled. They started to mess with the drunken man on the bench. I was a little mad I mean I found him first. But the boys were bigger than me so I let them have my bum. They took a brick and threw it at him. BAM! The man woke up and chased us. We were screaming and laughing at the same time. Then I heard her my mother who was looking out the window and called me upstairs. That's how she use to call us in by hanging out the window and yelling Rachel, Junior, Craig, Raif and we would say coming. I didn't want to go because I knew she would beat me and no one was home either that meant she would beat me until she got tired. Baby Doll came with me as we explained that I didn't have anything to do with it. That is was Pete and David. my mother just said go to your room and don't come out. I mumbled I hate you, and went to my room. She followed me and asked me what did you say. Boy was I scared my stomach was in a knot and I sure could have used the bathroom at this time. Think, think so I did what any child would do I lied and said I didn't say nothing. She sat on my bed and said, when I was a child my mother used to get me mad and make me go to my room, and I would mumble under my breath names to call her so tell me I'm not mad. What did you say? So again I lied and said, "You know I didn't do nothing". She said, "See that wasn't hard was it". Ah yeah I thought But, she had this look in her eyes. I knew that she knew I didn't say that. From that time on I lied about everything and anything. My brothers use to say stop "Racheling" so much instead of stop lying so much. Oh yeah my name is Rachel and I was born Friday the 13th. Isn't that something of all days to be born Friday the 13th.

I mean even God hated me or at least I thought so. I mean out of all the days I could have been born Friday the 13th at 12:03.

My block was real cool we had block parties where everyone would have food and fun we would ride bikes and dance. There were a lot of people living on Greene Ave. A lot of kids and fun my mother was lots of fun all the neighbors liked her and she use to sit on the stoop with her friends, talking and laughing. And dancing boy could my mother dance. Her favorite song was "Grazing in the Grass". Can you dig it. When they played that on the radio she would stand up and dance. And everyone would watch her. I just wish it would last forever. I mean the dance, but it didn't. The dance never is long enough is it?

One day we were playing outside and a boy named Charlie Brown was with us he was little like me I mean he was skinny and had a big head, really his name was Charlie Brown and just like Charlie Brown there was a sadness about him. His father was a hot headed man. He would play cards outside with the other men and if he was losing the whole block knew about it. He was loud with it. What I lost you bastards cheated me. Fuck this I'm not playing and I'm not paying either. What you gonna do about it. Yeah I thought so.

I thought he was cool a little loud but cool. Then one day I guess he didn't pay and someone opened his head with a base-ball bat. There was blood everywhere. Baby Doll and I said that's a lot of blood for a little head. And before we knew it there was no more Charlie Brown. That's the way it was. Everyone had their moments. My mothers moment came when she was pregnant and had a little girl name Kaneda Victoria. One day Kaneda went to the hospital with my father and when he came back she was not with him. My mother cried and I think she blamed my father for her death but she had pneumonia. Everyone has there moments. My little brother pushed over a gallon of water on my foot and I got five stitches and a cast. Everyone has there moments. Right. I mean there was the fighting and the arguing and on occasion there was a murder or two but the block was cool and I lived on it.

My block had a lot of children on it that I could play with. But only Baby Doll was my friend she had a lot of friends and since I was her friend they let me be with them. One day Baby Doll was not home she went to visit her brother in jail with her mother. So I was left with Renee. She likes this boy named Wade. He was so cute light skin and tall. Renee asked me to come with her and Wade to the hallway at her apartment and I did. She started kissing him and they were making all kinds of noises. I remember thinking what are they doing. And why are they doing it. And why am I here. When they were finish Renee said, "don't. tell anyone". Ok who would want to know anyway? But, as soon as Baby Doll came back I told her and any one who would want to listen. The next day my mother gave me money for an ice cream she always made sure we had Mr. Softee. Renee came marching up to the Mr. Softee truck she was mad as she could be. She asked me did I tell anyone what she did and I said, "No". Renee got even angrier, she knocked my ice cream out of my hand and said that I was a liar. All of a sudden I heard my mother yelling from the upstairs window, Rachel, Rachel come here. She wanted me to come upstairs I didn't know what my mother wanted and I couldn't think of a lie. Damn this is not fair what did I do. Walking up those stairs my heart was pounding. The sweat started forming on my upper lip. And my legs just started shaking, oh God what does she want. By time I got to my apartment door I was in tears. She opened the door and said, "What's going on". I looked puzzled I couldn't think of anything to say. She said, "What's going on downstairs that girl knocked your ice cream out of your hand." Oh that, what a relief I thought. Renee is mad at me and she doesn't like me. Before I could say anything else my mother had me by the arm and started dragging me down the stairs. She was saying if you don't kick her ass I'm gonna kick yours. I wanted to put on the brakes to this movie. You mean fight is she crazy. I can't fight, Renee is so big and she got boyfriends. I knew that I didn't want my mother's beating but I knew I didn't want Renee's either. When the door to the street opened I wanted it to close back before I knew it mom was in front of Renee saying that, "Rachel has something to say to you".

Ah yeah right I said, ah Renee don't knock down my ice cream again ok. Wow, that wasn't so bad. I turned to walk away and my mother stood in front of me and said, "kick her ass."

What?

What choice did I have then. So I did. I remember hitting Renee like mom hit me. Renee was crying and screaming I just keep hitting her. Boy the power of the punch. Then Renee's mother came out to break it up. Why did she do that? My mother grabs her and started beating her. They where fighting so hard that you could hear the punches. Renee and I stopped fighting and started watching them. My mother throws her on the ground and then picks her up and throws her in the back of my fathers white convertible car. Then my father came and got them out of the car. He sent my mother and me upstairs. As we were going upstairs my mother said, now that's how you fight. Do you understand?

I said, "Wow mom." Yeah I get it. Man I thought my mother kick my ass but she never kicked my ass like she kicked Renee's mothers. That night all we talked about was the fight, and every time I told it, it was different. But the ending was the same mom and I won.

The next day I was gleaming' I had a fight and that was all right. Then Bennie, a boy who lived in Renee's apartment building, said, "she's my cousin". But, back then all you needed was a like for another person and they where your "cousin". Well he came up to me after school and said, " I heard you beat up my cousin'."

I didn't say anything. He said I should beat you up. I still didn't say anything then he hit me. And I still didn't say anything. I guess I need my mother to threaten me so I could fight. I walked home and saw my father outside on the stoop. I said hi dad. He said, what happened to you I told him about Bennie and what happened after school. He said, "I'll pick you up after school tomorrow and you show me who Bennie is.

Yeah my Daddy. The next day couldn't come fast enough for me and the end of school couldn't either. I went outside and seen my DAD. Then I spotted Bennie. I said Bennie my Dad wants to talk to you. My daddy said did you hit my daughter and Bennie said yes.

My daddy said, "well you need to pick on someone your own size" and Bennie said "like you". Well before I knew it and to my surprise my daddy pushes Bennie and he landed on his butt. Everyone laughed. And so did I. That night we were eating dinner and a knock came on the door. It was the cops they wanted to speak with my DAD. I heard my mother yelling and my father saying I'll be back Pearl. I didn't know what happened and why. But she did. She grabbed me by the throat and lifted me right out of my seat. She keep saying this is your fault bitch. You know how you're in water and you go too deep in it and your feet can't touch the ground and you panic and can't breathe. Well, that's how I felt I started to get dizzy and my hand felt like little ants where running up and down them. She carried me to my room and when she released me I was afraid to breathe. She said, "don't come out of this room." I don't know if I fell asleep or passed out but when I awoke I still felt her hands around my throat. I mean I touch my neck and you could still feel her hand around my throat. The voice of my father talking in the hallway to my brothers was a joy to hear. But I didn't move. I learned to hold my pee that day, all day. Later that night my father said, do you want something to eat, come on out of this room.

The first stop was the bathroom. I was so nervous I started to shake and shake. My breathing was all over the place and in that little bathroom you can hear your heart beat so loud. Oh God should I get some food. Then I thought oh yeah my father is home. The next stop the food. I never knew what had happened that day and trust me I never asked.

Later that year the apartment next to us caught on fire and everyone had to move. We ended up at a hotel where we all had to sleep in the bed together. Mom also had another baby a little girl Vanessa and she was so pretty and tiny. My little sister. Then there were five of us, the Browns.

CHAPTER 2

Bones

We only stayed in the hotel for a little while my Daddy then got us a house in Queens. I didn't want to move to Queens it sounded like another country where they spoke another language or something.

When we moved to Queens I was the new girl in the classroom and on the block. I didn't know my way around and Daddy had to pick us up from school and Mommy would walk us. And just to make it clear having Daddy pick you up was ok. But, having mom take you was a drag, her feet hurt all the time and she complained all the time. It was like, damn, why you just didn't stay home we know how to get to school. This block was long I mean it had an alley way to divide the block that's how long it was. On one half of the alleyway attached houses and on the other side, where we lived, there were detached houses and we had a garage in our backyard. On this half of the block was Nelly, Linda and Barbara my best friends. Barbara lived with her Grandmother and Grandfather but there was no mother. I never knew what happened to her parents. And I never asked. Everyone thought we were sisters. Nelly was very light skinned and had a real handsome brother named Gerald. It was funny Nelly looked just like her mother fat and light skinned and Gerald looked like his father dark and handsome. Linda had four sisters and two brothers. And her mother was a happy women I mean always happy. Leslie and her brothers and sisters were happy people and they party all the time. Queens wasn't so bad.

After a while everyone knew us. I would go to school and everyone knew me I was loud and a liar. And my mother loved to go shopping. She would buy us all kinds of clothing real nice clothes. Especially after she would beat me to cover up the scares I guess she would buy me clothes.

Anyway.

So I was always well dressed with the latest styles. And it was cool with everyone. You see Queens was all about the fashion, and I was keeping up with the Jones. They started calling me Bones and I loved it. I had a nick name. I wasn't black and baldy anymore I was Bones.

Barbara also dressed real nice and her grandmother always would take her shopping for new clothes too. I thought wow she was getting beatings too. And that's what everyone I saw with new clothes, I thought they were getting beatings too. Wow Queens was cool.

Going to school was so cool. I learned a whole new form of lying. I would tell everyone that my father was my brother. My father had a way of looking young all the time. It's like he never aged. You know my father also keep getting better looking. At least that's what all the kids from the school would say. The girls would giggle when they seen my father and I used that to the best of my ability. The girls in the Junior High School was easy and I use to lie about everything. Bones, Yeah the liar and when you would ask me to confirm the lies I just back it up with another lie. Man I was getting so good with lying that I used to believe some of my own lies.

My home life didn't change much it was violent very, very violent and it was all reflected towards me. I started to notice that not everyone was getting beatings like me and maybe something was wrong with me. I used to think why my mother didn't like me. She used to beat me almost unconscious, and leave me bloody on the floor. And no one would help me. Not even my brothers, I mean no one.

Anyway.

Going to Junior High School 192 was in Hollis and it was the bomb back then. We had Rappers DJing outside in the schoolyard they used to be battling everyday with different MC's. I used to listen to the music and imagine that I was a big star and Diana Ross was my mother and I was in a different family. Everyday I used to cry. But through all the pain I was fly. And being fly meant something in Queens, even if your life didn't.

In class it was a breeze it seem like all the girls in the class were all Pisces like me. There was Michelle who had like 10 brothers and sisters, Fannie Mae Frazier who peed on herself every chance she got. Kim who no one liked because she was pretty and smart. So I was with Kim just in case that Barbara (who I named Babes) would not do my homework. Babes felt sorry for me because she knew my home life or lack of it. So she would help me with my work and homework. She also knew that my reading was not the best and everyday in her big bedroom she would give me something to read most likely the Right On magazine. It was all about the Jackson Five and I use to tear out the pictures and hang them on my wall in my room. Oh yeah and Max out of the Sunday paper. Max used to put beautiful pictures in the paper and you could color it yourself. Oh man I loved Max pictures and my Jackson Five.

Anyway back to the hood of things.

One day Fannie Mae peed in class and one of the girls started to make fun of her. They followed her into the hallway and tees her so bad that Fannie Mae would not or could not take it anymore. She turned around and grabbed girlfriend and started beating her like she needed to. I mean Fannie Mae was like Mohammad Ali that girl could fight. From that moment on you did not and would not make fun of Fannie Mae anymore. I mean you didn't even think of making fun of her even if she had pee running down her leg and it was dancing and singing in the isle. Michelle, Kim, Fannie Mae and me were a team. Kim and I did not have to fight because Fannie Mae and Michelle would fight for us. And that was all right with me. School was working out just like I've planned it. I mean if my mother beat me at home I would come to school find someone I didn't like and think of a good lie and set Fannie Mae and Michelle on "it"...

Until one day Fannie Mae got her a boyfriend a big ugly guy named Hank. I mean he was butt ugly, but so was Fannie Mae. I thought to myself who would name they child Hank. I could see Fannie Mae but not Hank. And they were a couple and she got pregnant. That was the end of us hanging out with Fannie Mae. You know being a 6th grader and pregnant did not fit well in school. So Fannie Mae had to leave the school. Later I heard that she had a boy and I thought, that was cool. But oh man who did he look like.

Kim also had a boyfriend he was real cute and both her and Michelle wanted him and he used it all the way. Playing one against each other. So I had to help my friends to get rid of Kim's cute boyfriend. There was this guy named Barry who I knew didn't like him so everyday I would tell Barry and his friends different things about Kim's boyfriend until they started to get pissed at him. They jumped him after school one day and we all know that pretty boys can't fight. My lie worked out just right the only thing I didn't count on is Kim and Michelle finding out that I told Barry and his friends a bunch of lies about their little boy toy. When they approached me with all the outrageous accusations I couldn't believe it. See both Kim and Michelle were pregnant by the cute guy and formed up against me. So I did what every kid would do when their best friends get mad at her I lied. I said, no way why would I say anything about him. Little did I know I was being set up they had the nerve to go to Barry and bring me along.

Ouch.

That really hurt. But, being the great liar that I was I just pulled out my special I got busted lies which work like this:

I looked Barry in the eye and said, No Barry you are mistaking you got that backwards and my favorite lie of all, "Ok if I said that, then what did I say." Knowing that no one could repeat what you said word for word so then when they started not getting it right my lies were there to correct them and confuse them. My lies were so good that Barry and his friends didn't want to even talk to us anymore about it. And when that happened like I knew it would. I said to Michelle and Kim, "see how they lied on me." My closing was Barry always liked me and he was just mad because I didn't like him. My lies where like a good movie you must see it again.

But, no matter what once your fiends know you lied even if they couldn't prove it they just aren't your friend anymore. I mean they would talk to me and we walked to class together but it just wasn't the same. Plus the baby thing they had to go. Now when your friend leaves you and you have no one left its time to go to class and start learning something. So I did I went to all me classes that whole week. I even decided to go to Art. When I walked in that class the teacher didn't know who I was I was cutting Art so much that I never even met the teacher. I thought of a good lie and said hey I would leave if you want me to, but then my education would be on your hands.

Damn that was good and I knew the teacher would fall for that. So I sat down and here I was. I had on a pleated black skirt and a beautiful pink puff sleeved blouse. The pink blouse had three buttons on the sleeves and a big collar. The skirt fitted me like a glove. See the day before my mother came home with these outfits for me. She had a Macys credit card. My mother had great taste in clothes. So I knew I was just the best dressed that day.

Anyway back to the Hood of thing:

After the art teacher called the office to confirm that I was in her class she sat me at the back by the door. I didn't want to sit in the front anyway. I guess she figured that I would not stay long anyway. She had this bowl of fruit on her desk and asked us to draw it she said that some famous artist started his career drawing fruit. How boring now I know why I didn't go to art. What a lie I thought teachers always do that lie so you would do their work. Like someone could have a career drawing fruit. Then there was a knock on the door. I looked at it, it was Felicia. Felicia was part of this group of girls who would take other girls bangles. There was Ginger the leader known for the fatness strumming from her big neck and nice clothes. Brenda the fat light skin girl that had a boyfriend named Patrice who everyone in the school liked and then there was Felicia whose head looked like it was too big for her body. But they were the best dressed girls in school & the fastest. And rumor had it that they made those clothes.

Anyway:

Felicia was at the door. I asked the teacher did she want me to open it. She said, yes. So I did. Felicia grabbed hold of my blouse and ripped the sleeve right off. I couldn't believe it my mother is going to kill me. Oh shit. What did she do that for you Bitch? What the. Then I shut the door. I looked at the teacher and she said maybe it was an accident. She really didn't mean it just stay calm and I will call the Principal. Yeah right I said Fuck that. I opened the door and went outside and there she was with Ginger and Brenda laughing and cheering like this was some kind of Got Damn prize to win. I looked at Felicia and she said; now your friends are not here what are you going to do Bones? I hit her so hard in her mouth that my hand hurt and I had to fight her left handed. I smashed her face into the glass case that was in the hallway with all the arts and crafts that other kids made and I was hoping that it broke but it didn't all I keep thinking about while I was whipping on her ass is that my mother was going to kill me. No I mean really kill me dead. Felicia managed to break free of my "Cleopatra Jones" grip. That's when I reached back and there it was a ruler the ones with the metal edged I had it in my left hand and I worked that like a glove. Felicia was screaming and I was cutting her ass up. Yeah. Then I notice that everyone started screaming. There was blood all over the place the Principal and Dean of Girls came and took her to the nurse and took me to the office. Man were they mad but they looked at me like I was a crazy person. They asked me where did I get the ruler and I said I don't know. They were like cops, but without badges and guns or cuffs. Well they thought they were like cops. Did you bring the ruler with you? Were your intention to harm her? And the one I hated the most was were you jealous of her? That one got my attention. See while they where questioning me I was singing. Rap. But when they said, jealous. I said why would you say that just because she looked better then me just because she dressed better then me just because I am black. I'm Bones and she's not jealous of no one. And I walked out. See I was Bones and I just cut up Felicia. Yeah I was feeling good that day. Until, school was over and when I saw the principal speaking to my father. Which all the kids said hey the Principal is speaking to you big brother! I went over there and Daddy asked me what happened I told him. I still had one sleeve and blood was all over my blouse and my right hand had swell by three o'clock. I told him everything. I loved my Dad and as long as he was going to be home that day everything would be cool it was Friday and daddy had to come to school with me Monday. So I had the whole weekend to tell my story. Babs loved it all the versions. Every time I told it, it changed one minute it was a ruler next minute a knife. Friday night Dad went to work and I was designing clothes for the Jackson Five in my room. My room was the sun porch. I had pictures of the Jackson Five hanging all over. They were so cool. Out of Sight. I use to sit and design clothes for the Jackson Five new pants for Michael and new costumes for the group. I thought my designs were really good and one day the Jackson Five would get stuck in front of the house and they would need some clothes and that's where I would come in. Then all of a sudden I felt something was wrong the house was too quiet and before I knew it my mother was there and she told my brothers to take down all the stuff off my wall. And they did the rip and rip and rip everything off my wall and then they left they looked like they really enjoyed it. I wasn't mad at the time they were only doing what she told them to do. Then I looked up at my mother who stood there with such great satisfaction in her face. She made a fist. I braced myself. Then she hit me right in the face. I looked at her she smiled and left. I hated that bitch. I wanted her dead. I didn't say a word I couldn't say a word I just went to sleep.

The next morning I awaken to pain I knew who it was I just didn't know what it was. I could hear her swinging. I just laid there not moving not saying a word. Then she stopped, maybe because I was not moving or saying a word, maybe she thought she finally killed me. I looked at her and she was standing there with a belt and the belt buckle was dripping blood off it. She look like she was out of breath and her glasses had fog on them I don't know where she got the belt from but when I find it. It's history. She said now go to the store and get me some bread. I had no choice. I never had a choice, **life is bad when you don't have a choice.** See she was my mother. And I did what she said. When she left I touched my head it was bleeding clots, my hair was red. She had stopped allowing me to take a bath in her house. But when my father was there I could. But not today. I got dressed put on my hat and was ready to go to the store. I knew to sit in the room until she called me. Just then my little sister came in while I was wiping some blood off my neck with my pillow case, she was so cute and she had big eyes too. She loved me and I loved her. She looked at me with her big eyes like she wanted to tell me something. And at that moment I think I knew what she wanted to say. But, she never said a word she just gave me a hug. As we were hugging a strange feeling came over me like I couldn't breath. Her hugging me made me want to cry. See I stopped crying over the beatings a long time ago. I used to act like I was crying so she would stop beating me. And I was good at acting like I was crying. But, holding my sister in my arms and feeling her little heart beat against mine made me feel like, like I don't know.

Anyway:

I told her that I was ok and that everything is alright. My little sister was the most important thing in my life. She used to sit on my bed and look at my designs. I was nine years older then her. And as a little sister she was the tops.

Well, my mother called me I went in her room she had this big round bed fit for a queen. My father treated her like a queen too. He would work three jobs and give her all his money. And she would spend every dime.

Anyway:

I took the money and stopped by Babs' house and we started to go, the queen wanted bread. I had on a flowered hat so that the blood wouldn't be seen. We went in the store and I thought about what would happen if I started bleeding all over this place. Joe that was the guy behind the counters name. Joe owned the store on the corner he was a fat white guy whose hair looked dirty all the time. Joe probably would say stop bleeding on my things and get out. Hey before you leave clean that mess up. Yeah that's probably what he would say. Alone again I began to think no one cared. I mean I wish there was a superman that would come and save me.

Anyway:

We got the bread and I put the change in the bag and started walking back home. In front of my house Barbara asked me if I could come outside, I told her no. She said well good luck Monday. I just wanted to disappear. That was the longest weekend of my life. I couldn't go outside so I came up with a great scheme. I would stay up all night and not go to sleep that means that Monday wouldn't come. I knew that would work. So I sat up doing my designs and playing with my paper people. I didn't have dolls but that was ok with me I've learned to make my own dolls and dress them like I wanted to. I started picking some of the blood out of my hair but it dried up and well it hurt. Well to my surprise Monday came all I thought about was bloody Monday. The day my mother was coming to the school. As we walked to the school my mother was complaining that her feet were hurting and she cursed every step. That was satisfying to me I was glad her feet hurt. How did she think I felt? I was the one with the hat on to cover up all that blood. Before we got to school she said don't tell them what happened to your head. I just looked at her she said did you hear me. I said yeah I heard you. We got to the school and had to wait for the Principal and Dean of Girls. It felt like hours. Then they called us in. Felicia and her mother were there. Her mother was light skin like her and had big pink lips. They almost had on the same outfit. Skirt and jacket. My mother and I hand on pants. Felicia has a scar on her face and they say she had stitches on her arm. I felt great. The Dean of Girls had a file on me that looks like a book. They showed my mother all the things I've done and that I was absent more then I was there. My mother looked uninterested about that. Then they started about the fight. Telling her that I cut her with a ruler and kept cutting her like I was under a spell. Felicia's mother said, that "she had to go to the hospital and was under a lot of pain all weekend." I smiled. Then to my amazement and everybody that was there my mother spoke. Wow she started saying that she didn't care about what I've done. And the bitch rips a blouse that she bought. And if Felicia learned to fight she wouldn't have got her ass kicked. She would know now that she won't fuck with Rachel no more won't she. Oh wow. What a speech you go mom. The principal said Ms. Brown that was not the point. And my mother said, "I was talking." That is the point if the girl would have done that to my daughter you wouldn't have said shit. Felicia's mother said, "Well I want you to pay for the doctors' bill."

I thought if I were her I wouldn't have said that. My mother respond by "I ain't paying shit. Now I'm going home and my feet are hurting. Don't call me no more about this shit". And she walked out.

All of us were still sitting there we couldn't believe it. Then my stomach started to move inside and my arms and feet start to shake and I bust out laughing. I mean I laughed so hard I almost peed on myself. As I walk to class I was still laughing. After school a boy walked up to me. He looked familiar and then I knew he was the boy who gave me the ruler. He had hazel brown eyes light skinned and very good looking he wore a gene jacket with the "Skulls" colors on it. His name was Tyberius, Ty was a member of a gang named the Savage Skulls. They ran Hollis and part of Linden Blvd & Murdock up to O'Connell Park. I asked him why did you give me the ruler and what's up with that.

He asked me my name I said, "Bones." He looked me up and down and said cool. As we walked home he explained that Felicia's boyfriend used to be a member of the Skulls and quit that was not cool. He was going to beat her up but when he saw me fighting her, he thought that this would be a good time to get her. Cool. We walked to my house and everyone knew him. It must have taking hours to get there. He had to stop off and speak to a lot of people (all girls). When we finally got to my block it was like he was a star everyone looked at me and I know they wanted to ask me about Tyberius, and I ate it up. When we got to Babs' she was outside wanting to know about what happened at school today.

Boy did I tell lies I made my mother sound like Bruce Lee in Enter the Dragon. You know while she was not fighting like Bruce Lee. Her words where a big karate kick.

Tyberius loved my story and I loved talking about it. By time we got to my house my brother Craig was on the stoop. Babs and Tyberius sat on the stoop with him while I went in the house to see the mood my mother was in. I listened to the door and I didn't hear her breathing on the other side, so I went in.

My brother Craig was real quiet he had big eyes and big ears and he loved to wiggle those ears and everyone loved to watch him wiggle them. Craig was the middle boy. He had sickle cell anemia and was always sick, but if you looked at him you would never know it.

Anyway back to the Hood of things:

She was happy and act like nothing was wrong. I told her that Tyberius was outside and she wanted to see him. I guess number one; I never bought a boy home before & number two the name Tyberius makes you want to meet him.

I mean really doesn't the name Tyberius make you want to meet him?

When she saw him oh when she saw him. He was sitting down and he turned around to meet her. His eyes shined in the sunlight they almost look like glass. He wasn't a tall man but for our age, I mean we were in 8ᵗʰ grade, he was tall enough. When he smiled he had dimples and honey brown skin. But he had a look that let you know don't fuck with me. I said this is my mother Mrs. Brown. He stood up and said hi. She smiled and said hi. Then he said I heard about what happened at school today. I stopped breathing and was hoping that he wouldn't repeat the lies I told him, but he didn't. My mother was so proud of what she did that she started telling her story herself. While Craig, Babs, Tyberius and me listened. Her story was not as exciting as mine. And I guess Babs and Tyberius was wondering about it. I mean her story wasn't even as long as mine. Babs and Tyberius knew I lied by now but neither one of them said anything about it. Then came the hard part. My mother asked him what is that on his jacket. He told her that he was in a gang and the name was The Savage Skulls. I thought she would hit the roof but she didn't she act like nothing was wrong with it. And so did all of us. You see it was nothing wrong with it there were gangs everywhere. There was the Ace of Spades from Linden to Farmers. The "Hollis Crew" they only had Hollis Ave. the "South Side Boys" they were in the South Jamaica and then the "Baisely Boys" who had the Baisely Project.So you see they where everywhere. Tyberius needed to use the phone and my mother said ok. I took him to the phone which was located between the living room and my room (the sun porch). I took this time to show him my room. It had a bed and dresser. Then I pulled out my paper people and designs. He though that my designs where cool. But he didn't understand the paper people. We went back outside and joined the others. He really liked my brother Craig and I could tell that Craig really liked him. As we sat on the stoop getting to know each other and laugh about the stories that Tyberius would tell us. He told us stories about fighting and stealing cars. I was all in. Then a car pulled up and a dark skin guy named "Spinner" came to the stoop. Every step he took another breath. He was handsome. He was tall dark and handsome and I wanted him to be my boyfriend. And every chance I got I tried to convince him to be my boyfriend.

Anyway Back to the Hood of Things:

Tyberius had to go, but before he left he introduced us to Spinner, one of the members of the Skulls. Then he said he would see us later and made a sound like chow, chow, chow. And then they where gone. The week went by and I didn't see or hear from them. On Saturday morning we heard a sound chow, chow, chow. I ran to the window and there he was with a smile on his face. I asked my mother could I go outside that Tyberius was there she said yeah. I yelled out the window I'm coming. I put on my panties, jeans and tee shirt and also my flowered hat. My mother still wouldn't let me take a shower.

I had a smile on my face when I saw him. I couldn't believe it he came back to see me. Why? Who cares why he came back to see me? As we started walking towards Linden Blvd. He asked me, "Why are you wearing that hat?" I felt like running away, but I didn't, I looked at him and said, "because my mother hit me in the head with a belt buckle and she wouldn't let me wash the blood out of my hair". Then I showed my shoulders and looked at him. We stopped in the middle of the street he said, "let me see."

I thought ok this guys crazy. He just want to laugh at me, but he has an angry look in his hazel eyes. I should not have told him

I thought. Now look I'm in the middle of the street and he wants to see the bloody, bald head. I knew that if he seen my bald spot and nappy hair that was still stained with blood I was afraid that he would send me right back home. And maybe worse he wouldn't want to be my friend and that's something I couldn't do. My heart started beating fast and I had no choice so I took it off. He went behind me and touched it. He said, you know you should get stitches. Hey it's still bleeding. I just wish he would get from back there. He said, "you still have blood in you hair". So I said, what are you a doctor. He laughed a little and said, "Here's your hat." We continue to walk we stop at a store and Tyberius took food and oj and did not pay for it. When we got out of the store I said, "Do you know him in the store?"

He said, "No I just don't pay for anything that I could steal."

He stopped, looked at me and smiled and said, "because Bones I steal. Ok. Anymore questions or do you want some."

Yeah, "Where the hell are we going!" He stopped and said I'm taking you to the hospital. I didn't question him again.

I just took the o j and cinnamon bun and kept getting up. Wow stealing that's cool don't pay for anything you can steal. That's a keeper. We went to Farmers blvd. right around the corner from the bank. There was this house with a green fence around it. It was a small house with only one floor. I never seen a house so small. Tyberius didn't even knock he just went in. I followed him and he turned to me and said, " have a seat."

I sat down on a brown flowered couch. There was also a table I guess it was the dinning room, and there where pictures all over the place. I mean pictures of people a lot of people. Kids, men, women with kids some had on uniforms like in the Army. I wonder who are all these people. Then two girls came out with their bathrobes on and I wondered what was Tyberius doing and where is he. They were dark skinned just like me but they had a sense of confidence., and they had nice teeth. Their teeth shined like diamonds. Their hair was in curlers and I looked down one of them was bare footed and she had her toe nails painted red. The other one had slippers on and they had little roses on the toes and was pink. The pink slippers also matched her pink Chinese bathrobe. I thought wow who are these girls, and where is Tyberius. Finally he came out from the back. With another girl and she was hugging all over him. I just wanted to leave. I no longer wanted to stay at this house.

Tyberius looked at me and said, "Hey Delores look at the scare in the back of Bones head."

She said, "Your name is Bones?"

The girls looked at me and I guess they agreed Bones it is.

I said, "Delores or what ever your name is Do Not Put Your Hands On Me."

I'm showing you nothing.

Come on Tyberius I'm ready to go. I don't know if I was upset because he did this to me. Or, because I trusted him and now look. I felt like a freak from the circus but I sucked it up and said, "let's go!"

He came over to me and said, "Bones it's ok they will help you that's why I brought you over here".

"I don't want their help" I yelled.

"But can you do if for me please" Tyberius said.

Looking at him into those eyes he looked like he really wanted to help me and all those girls standing around I said ok. I took off my hat Delores got a chair and said here sit down so I can see real good. So I did. Delores said wow that is a big gash and you should go to the hospital and get it looked at.

Tyberius said, "she can't go that's why I bought her here. See her mother did that with a belt buckle."

Well I could have died when he said that. Then Delores said that's ok we'll take care of it she continue to wash it and comb it. They got a towel and put it around my shoulder. I didn't know that it was still bleeding. She said, this is going to hurt. I said why?

She added iodine and it stung but I didn't let her know. But I was strong and felt brave. She really worked on my head for a long time. Then got all the blood out and was able to run a comb through it. She even controlled the bleeding. I know because I didn't see anymore blood come out of the comb. Then she greased it and started to corn roll my hair straight back. She smelled real good. I asked her what is that smell she said Tabu it's a perfume and I wear it all the time. Note to self get some Tabu. After my hair was done I help them clean up. There was a lot of blood in a bucket. And I went through three towels. I asked where are your parents. She said her daddy was in jail for bank robbery. And her mother is a nurse at Kings County Hospital in Brooklyn. I said are you all sisters? She said no these are my cousins. I wanted to ask if that girl was seeing Tyberius but I didn't. Tyberius said let me take the garbage out and I will see you girls later. I was so thankful I said yeah I'll see you later. Then we left. I felt good walking down the street with Tyberius and my new hairstyle. When we got to my house Tyberius said he was going home and will see me later. I said where are you taking the garbage do you want me to dump it out. He said no I'm gonna burn it so you would never see it again ok. I felt so proud of him. He's wonderful. I said see yah later. Then I tried the front door but no one was home. I went to the back door and it was unlock like always so I went in. There was no one home. But, that was not unusual sometimes only us kids where home or sometimes it was just mom or just dad home. It was something that happens. I was sitting in my room when they came home. I heard one of my brothers saying she's home. I went to help with the groceries my father had in the station wagon and you can put a lot of groceries in there. And we had a lot. I mean with five kids there where a lot of things to buy. When I started back to my room just to remember the good day I had.

My mother called me and said, where were you. I said I went with Tyberius. I started to finish telling her about the hospital and Delores and her cousins. But she cut me off and said, I didn't tell you to go anywhere.

I couldn't believe this. I said, in my defense you said I could go outside.

She said, bitch I said you could go on the stoop.

Now wait I remember her saying I could go outside nothing about the stoop.

She said, "we looked all over for you."

I looked around the room and my brothers and sister were looking at me like yeah we were looking for you. My father came in to join us. I knew that he wouldn't be arguing at me. But this day to my surprise he was. They gang up on me one was saying that you can't go outside today. You never listen and I'm tired of you the other would say. Then my mother asked me who you want to beat you me or your father. Ok this is a no brainer.

I said with pride, "Daddy."

Then my mother said, "ok we'll both beat you".

Ok what is wrong with this picture was she angry at me because my hair was done. Was she upset because I finally got the blood out of my hair. What is wrong with this picture. I knew that she had to have her hand in beating me. But that day with my father looking at me. I decide to show them I will not cry today. No matter what. Why didn't she like me? Why didn't she love me? And why did he get involved. I thought he would help me, I thought he of all people he would be on my side. But he wasn't my father the man that I needed in my life. And he let me down. I just thought if he knew that she was beating me like this he would do something. Oh what is going on. She started first and when she swung I blocked it. Boy did that get her pissed. But, I keep blocking it. I was really tired of being her punching bag. Then my father started to grab me and I moved back then we both were surprised. Yes I was not going to take it anymore. Well my father tried to grab me again and ripped my tee shirt, I couldn't believe it. What was going on? I could tell that they were getting tired. I was blocking and moving. Yeah it's hard to hit a moving target isn't it? My brother I'm not sure which one said it but he said start crying and they will stop. Then my mother caught me off guard and punched me right in my face.

But I was tired of that making believe that I was crying by putting spit on my cheeks to make the tears and making that awful sound of crying. Then my father punched me in the stomach and when I bent down my mother was all over me hitting me in the back. I know I should have started crying but it was just so "done". So I didn't my mother said she hit me. But I know I didn't. When she said that I lost my control of the beating and my dad had me he hit me with his hand but it didn't hurt. Then he said, go to your room and don't come out for the rest of the day. I felt like a champion. No like a Skull yeah a Skull. I went in my room and imagined that I was the leader of the Skulls and no one would hit me.

Anymore.

That night I was sleep. I felt that I couldn't breathe, I was trying to fight but something was over my face. I couldn't see and I was losing. I struggled, but I couldn't get my breath. Then when I started to accept that I was dying, air came back I coughed and looked around and my mother was standing there with the pillow in her hand.

She said, see bitch I could have got you. Then she threw the pillow at me and left.

The next day I got up, got dress and went to Babs house. She had her cousin Karen there. Karen was from Harlem and knew one of the singers from Black Marble. She was light skinned and she thought she was all that I mean yeah she looked nice but give me a brake all that she wasn't. She wanted me to come with her to Harlem to her aunt's house. I knew I had to ask my mother. So we started our long walk to my house. I just knew she would say no. But Karen said she would ask for me. I thought a no is a no. Karen went into my house and Babs and I followed. My mother was in a good mood. Oh I see my father is still home.

They act like nothing happened yesterday. And my mother must have forgotten that she tried to kill me.

When my father was home mom and him used to go in their room and when mom would come out she was in a good mood. I never knew what they did but I was glad they did it.

Anyway.

Karen asked mom could she take me with her and Babs to Harlem. My mother said, where in Harlem. Karen said 129th right off St. Nicholas. My mother said that she use to live on 135th street. I thought I didn't know that. But I didn't know a lot about my mother. She never talks to me about her life hell about

Anything.

She said yes as long as we came back before nighttime. Karen promised her she would have us home in time. Then we went on the longest journey ever. We took a bus to the Avenue. Then took the E train to 42nd St. Then had to wait for the A train to 125th St. Then we walked the longest dirtiest street ever. Harlem was filthy the ground seem like mud was on it. And that smell like oh that smell. It was the buses or the drunken man sleeping on the ground. Whatever it was it was bad. It was crowded with people. I mean a lot of people. There were black men with big hats and rainbow shoes. They all look like pimps from the movies. The women looked tired like they lived a hard life. There were tall buildings like Brooklyn but unlike Brooklyn there were stores everywhere. Then we finally got to the building where Karen lived. As soon as the door opened we only walked up one flight of stairs, and then I smelled it, an old familiar smell like burnt feet. And then I thought yeah this is just like Brooklyn. She was not no different than me she was just light skin. We went into her apartment And all you heard was the plastic from the couch. It was sticky and when you have on hot pants it was uncomfortable. The whole family was there except for her father. Who was a Black Panther and they didn't stick around long you know.

I wasn't sure that her father was a Black Panther but whatever he wasn't there. There were pictures of Martin Luther King and Malcolm X in velvet. Her mom was cool. She spoke like she was high on something then I learned that her mother smokes weed. And trust me she looked like it with her red eyes. I thought to myself another say it loud I'm black and proud moment. They didn't eat pork so we had soup. It was good. But I wanted to see Harlem and not sweat my ass off on some plastic. Then he walked in one of the members from the music group, The Black Marble, the dark skin one. He had on a dashiki and jeans. I was in love but he was Karen's boyfriend and there was no way that a man like that could pick a black bald girl over her. The Black Marble was a new group of three. They had a green eyed guy who sings really high and the other two was his back up singers. Man that music group. I really met one of the Black Marble. While we were there I keep checking the door to see if the other two would come over oh yeah maybe they would do a song. Oh that would be cool. A song.

Well Back to the Hood of Things.

They started to talk to me and Babs. They asked us did we know our true selves. What? They must be high. Then they started to explain they were in a movement for the people. That they were dealing with the Honorable Elijah Muhammad. And that "you sisters should come to the meeting". I thought to myself, there's no way that I'm going to any meeting for "the people". What people? They are bugging. But Babs seem to like it. She said, that she would go. We went to a place on 125th St. where the women sat on one side and the men on another. I hated it. They were all dress real funny and boy did they have kids. The kids where everywhere. Some women had on white and things on their heads and long skirts and their face was not shown. I remember thinking boy are they hot or what. I didn't hear a word they said I just kept blocking it out. I wanted to go back to Queens.

After whoever spoke everybody got up and left. Yeah we were leaving. I was ready to go but no, we had to stand there and speak about how good the speaker spoke. Then Babs who act like she was possessed by it, started to talk about how she was going to be more involved or something like that I just keep going towards the train station. The A train never looked so good. But no we had to stop at Shabazz for a Philly style steak. I didn't have any money. I mean how rude is it to just go to a restaurant and didn't ask anyone did they have any money. But I guess since he was with the Black Marble maybe he would pay for all of us. But No. So Babs shared hers with me. She was always good for that. We shared cupcakes and food all the time. She even one day shared her money by buying me a soda. I could always count on Babs to share with me. And that made me smile. She never asked me do I have money she just would buy enough for both of us.

The more that guy talked the more Babs and Karen listened. And the more I didn't. I could see that Babs was really into it. So I tried to act like I was into it too. But, Babs knew I wasn't . She kept hitting me under the table when I would sigh or roll my eyes. And I just looked at her like let's go. Then he started to talk to me.

Hey my Nubian' sister. With your natural black skin you should be doing more then running around with some gang.

Oh no he didn't. I said, "you don't know what you are talking about and if I was you I wouldn't say anything else about me or who I run with."

He said, "calm down sister I was just saying."

Oh yeah well I'm not your sister.

"You are in the dark and I'm just trying to put you in the light", he said.

Peace.

Yeah right peace I knew what that meant. I think I didn't like what he was saying because I didn't know what he was saying. He spoke about Angela Davis and when he did that I listened to him she was the ultimate black woman. Then he had the nerve to say that we as black women should submit to the black man. Ok I started blocking him out again. We sat there so long that the food was gone. And everyone knows that when the food is gone it's time to go. But no he keeps talking. On how we where lost in the wilderness. I just wanted to leave. And to my surprise yeah we left. Babs and I got on the A train and all she talked about was becoming a Muslim. I just wanted to be a SKULLette. It was longer getting home than going with her talking about lost in the wilderness and being a Muslim. I just sat there and said nothing. Then we were at 165ᵗʰ street. Yeah Queens where everyone was either in a gang or suckers. And I loved it. We walked home from there. I was so glad to see my street. I could have kiss the ground. I went home and everyone was playing outside. My mother was there and she didn't say anything about me taking so long. I went in my room and fell asleep. The next day I found out that there were new people living on the block. The Johnson's. They had two girls named Rinnie and Brenda. We called her burned to death because of her red hair. Rinnie was fat and black. And she was a bitch. Then there were two boys Junior and Keith. Junior was tall like Frankenstein. And Keith was short not bad looking. But, I knew that when they moved here it was trouble they came from the Bronx. And every word that thy spoke was The Bronx this and the Bronx that. Who cares about the Bronx? Not me. Because at this time I was one of the best fighters in Queens or at least I thought so. I use to fight everyday just to fight. I really enjoyed it. The pain of hurting your hand on someone's teeth, the way your heart would beat after 15 minutes of fighting. And oh yeah don't forget the blood. Not your blood the other persons blood. I enjoyed a good fight. And it was even more enjoyable when that person could fight also.

Anyway Back to the Hood of things.

One day I had a fight in the school yard. By this time it was known that I could fight, and when you could fight it was like being the fastest gun in the west everyone wanted a turn to take you out.

There was this girl from Francis Lewis Blvd. The girls came through the school yard. Oh yeah that was another thing walking through someone else's turf. That was a no, no. But, if you wanted to fight then that was a good way of doing it.

I was playing handball. And there they where three of them. Francis Lewis girls. She just started calling me out. Yo Bones I'm here.

I turned and said ok best man hit. Best man hit where a girl would stand in the middle of the two fighters and put her hand out then one of you would hit it. That's best man hit. And it was on.

I really like the way I would fight. I had the ability of being able to take you from one place to another just by one punch. She was bouncing off the hand ball court. And it was funny but when I had her on the ground and usually I would stomp you but this time I just wanted to punch her and she moved out of the way and I bust my hand. Oh shit did that hurt. After my girls stopped the fight, Tyberius came over he said, "what happened," holding my hand.

He seemed to be mad at me. I told him I didn't start this they came to me. He just interrupts me and said you should know better than that. You're not a good fighter just because you're a good fighter. You're a good fighter when you can pick your own battles and know when not to fight. Now let me see your hand.

I showed him my hand. Tyberius and I've gotten real close I told him everything. And when he wasn't around I missed him. His approval was all I lived for.

"See your hand if someone came to fight you now what would you do," he asked. I started to answer then he cut me off again. Nothing that's what you'll do. Let's go to the hospital and get you patched up. On our way to the hospital I asked him where has he been. He said, "no where."

I said but I haven't seen you in a month.

He said, "Don't worry about it."

Oh no was he angry at me, I felt the pit of my stomach turned. I had to think fast. He was walking fast and not talking. I didn't want him mad at me. So I told hem about Harlem and the Muslims. He was very interested in it. So then I told him my, you know I lied a lot to make the story seemed better. I made him laugh and I liked that.

He said, "I'm mad at you because you've been having a lot of fights lately and I don't want you to do that, I just want you to."

I looked into those hazel eyes and said, "What?" He never answered we where in front of the hospital. Delores answered the door.

And Tyberius said, "What can you do about this hand?" she looked at me and smiled.

She said, "welcome back Bones."

I can't do nothing but put some ice on it and let it heal. They started talking to him about what happened last month and they were sorry about his friend who got killed.

I couldn't believe it killed, killed someone got killed? Oh please not Spinner. Tyberius said, yeah that he and Spinner ended up in Spofford. And he just got out yesterday. Spofford was a jail where young cool kids went there it was in the Bronx. Then he was looking out his window and he sees Bones fighting. Can you believe it on my first day home Bones.

Delores said, "don't be mad at her she just wants to be like you." I felt like the child and they where my parents. Oh man would that be cool. He walked me home and his brother Tycus was on "Burnt to deaths" stoop.

Hey Tyberius isn't that your brother with Burnt to death? Tyberius went over there. So I did too. They were laughing and joking and I hated it. When his brother introduce Tyberius they were so happy. I knew his eyes would get them. Then everyday after that I used to go see Tyberius at Burnt to deaths house. I asked him what are you doing over here. He said they like giving it up. I thought giving what up?

What the fuck is giving it up? Burnt to death's brother started to like me or something I don't know. But at the last day of Junior High School 192 burnt to Death's little brother started picking on me and with my bad hand I couldn't make a fist. I mean I could fight him with my left hand but why is this boy always bothering me. So I decided not to fight him. As we walked through the school yard Tyberius was there. I told him that he was picking on me and I couldn't make a fist to fight him. Tyberius had on his colors and his dog chain and lock around his neck. I haven't seen him in full uniform in a long time. And when he was in full uniform he had the big thick dog chain around his neck. Tyberius walked right up to him and said, are you picking on my little sister. Burnt to Death's brother said, yeah. With a smile on his face. Like he was proud of it. Before he could say anything else Tyberius took off his chain and started whipping him with it. It was bad, I wanted Tyberius to stop. It wasn't that bad where he had to be beaten like that. I tried to tell Tyberius but he kept on hitting him, and Keith (Burnt to Death's brother) was screaming, you could hear the chain hitting him. It was bad. Then Spinner came with full colors also. I started to go to him and tell him to stop Tyberius but, he didn't bother to ask what was going on he just helped Tyberius stomp him. I couldn't wait for it to be over and them to leave. I mean I loved Tyberius and Spinner but all the blood just was making me sick. When they left Keith ran home. I wonder what where they doing there in full colors. And when they left they didn't say anything to me they just left. I walked home and I really wanted to go to speak to Keith and to ask him was he ok, but I couldn't I felt like it was all my fault. Maybe if I didn't tell Tyberius this wouldn't have happened. So I just went in the house and hope that he was ok.

Well **Back to the Hood of things**.

As if this day wasn't' bad enough my father was a security guard at the elementary school and on the last day of school for them he had to stay in till everyone left. When he was leaving he got in a fight with the Ace of Spades, another gang, four of them. When I heard about this I knew when Tyberius and Spinner had on colors it was because the Ace of Spades crossed their turf. My father told me and my brothers that they tried to get in the school and he wouldn't let them. So they started fighting. All day we kept seeing the Ace of Spades walking by our house. I was scared. Then Tyberius came over with a car of guys and Spinner. They asked daddy what happened. He told them and they left. The Ace of Spades never walked down our block again. And we didn't see Tyberius no more.

During that summer waiting to go to high school, Andrew Jackson, I was so excited. We also found out that Burnt to Death and her sister were pregnant by get this Tyberius and his brother. Babs was getting heavy into the Muslim thing and I had no one to play with. One weekend my brother, George Jr., got a new Fuji bike, it was red. And I wanted to ride it. I woke up early that morning and took the bike I went to 200 St and they were playing foot ball. Our foot ball was a little different. You had four people on the bike and four people on foot. The people on the bike would catch the ball and run for the touch down. The people on foot would tackle them. Everything was going right until I got tackled. I felt my leg snap and I went down.

When I got up I said I'm hurt and I'm going home. As I was riding home. It got harder and harder to peddle. My right leg just wouldn't move anymore the pain was really strong. Some guys on their bike road with me. By the time I got to my block I was peddling with one leg and the pain was so great that it was in my head. When I got home my brother said hey you took my bike. All he wanted was his bike back. When I got off that bike with one leg and hopped down, I hopped into bed and stayed there. Oh my leg was hurting. It would hurt if I thought about it. I couldn't move it or even think about moving it. I just stayed in bed all day, crying to myself. The next day my brother noticed that his bike was snap in half. And that I must have broken it. He told my father. When my father came in the room to yell at me about what happened to Junior's bike, I told him that we were playing football. My father started staring at me and then he said, why aren't you outside. I told him that I was a little tired. He said a little tired?

See it wasn't' like me to not be outside. Then he moved the blanket off of me. He said you still wearing the same close as of yesterday. I said, "oh I just didn't feel like getting undressed". Then a tear came down my cheek. A real tear not spit that I put there. He said what's wrong. My father really looked scared and wanted to know what was wrong with me. I told him that my leg hurt but I'll be alright. He said where does your leg hurt? I point to my knee and said right here. By this time Craig and Junior and Vanessa were there looking at me. Vanessa looked so scared. I smiled and told her I'll be ok. My father ripped my pants leg off. My green mustang pants he rip my green mustang pants. Man. And then my knee shot up. The pain was so great that I screamed out. My father picked me up and took me in his arms. And off to the car we went. My brothers and sister got in. He said, I'm taking you to the hospital. I thought wow he knows Delores too. Cool because Delores would know just what to do. Man I thought my father was real cool. Ah not Delores house we went to the real hospital, where real doctors and nurses where. When we got there my brothers and sister jumped out the car. My father picked me up and carried me in. He said I need a doctor my daughter needs a doctor. Help someone I need a doctor! My father was really scared and that made me scared too. All of a sudden my leg started really hurting. My leg had water in it the doctor said it was fractured. I thought that all I needed was a bandage and send me home. But no he had this big needle I looked at my father and he said to the doctor can you give her something for the pain. The doctor said it will go fast just hold on to her and the pain will not last long. And then he stuck it straight in my knee, it didn't hurt, but when he pulled the liquid out "oh the pain". The needle had a tube at the end of it and the liquid went into a bucket. After that the doctor put a cast on my leg and gave me and my brothers and sister a lollypop. A lemon lollypop. Not a cherry on a lemon one. My father got the crutches, and I went to the car. When we got home I couldn't wait to see Tyberius to show him my cast man will he be "syked". That summer I no longer saw Tyberius I didn't know where he was and with a cast on my leg I couldn't get far enough to find out. Babs became a Muslim and was hanging in Harlem a lot. Every time I saw her she was saying my sister you should do this and my sister you should do that. That was the last time I saw her. The last time I was on the block and the end of Bones.

CHAPTER 3

Gi - Gi

We moved that summer to Mangin Avenue a wide street about four blocks long, with the train track in the back. I had a broken leg and my parents gave me the basement as my bedroom. It had it's own door to go in and out and it's own bathroom. It was like an apartment. I loved it. But getting up and down the stairs with a cast on your leg and crutches was no joke. It was hard the stairs were narrow and it was a turn to make by the door to go down stairs. I really was sick of being like that. My brothers started to get taller and my little sister was still little but getting taller too. My little brother started to get the brunt of my mothers rage. She use to beat him and choke him. Like she use to do to me. He really took it hard and there was nothing I could do. But my father I think got tired of it all. He and my mother started to fight all the time. And I think it was her money spending and beating his children.

Anyway.

Having a broken leg and the new kid on the block did not suit me at all. Then my sister wanted me to meet this girl named Sheila. I tell you my sister had no problems meeting people and getting friends. So I got my crutches and hopped down the block with my sister guiding the way. She was so proud of me being her big sister that she had to show me off. We went down to the Banks house.

The Banks had about seven kids. Boys and girls. They were in the basement. It would be a basement! Man why couldn't anyone live on the ground level. When the door opened it was loud all the kids were making all this noise and in the middle of it was a light skinned girl with long black hair. It was Sheila. I thought she was crazy to be with all these kids. She stood up and she had tits. I never seen a girl my age with tits before and I couldn't help looking at them.

I said, "hi my name is Gi-Gi". How could you tell a girl with all these "titties" your name is bones, and I had to come up with something fast the only name I could think of was Gi-Gi from To Sir With Love. And she said, "hi I'm Sheila."

Then she walked outside with me. She showed me where she lived with her mother who's name also was Sheila. And here little brother named Gordon. All the houses were the same size a basement, attic, three bedrooms, a living room, dinning room and a kitchen. All were just the same. But everyone did it different. My mother had me in the basement. The Banks had a family room in the basement. And Sheila had a washer and dryer room in the basement. Sheila was funny like Carol Burnette. She knew everyone. I mean she knew boys and girls. She went to Jamaica High. Which was one of the best High Schools in Queens. While I went to Andrew Jackson. She was smart and I wasn't. She was light skin, and I was dark. Her hair was long and straight and my hair was short and nappy, but I liked her from that day one. She was honest and full of life. And that was good for me.

One day I was sitting on the stoop like I always did with my bad leg. And two guys came up the hill. We lived at the top of the hill. And everyone came our way. Like Mohammad a short guy with glasses and very well dressed, and Michael not any relation to us. He was tall and had red hair and light skin. They just came over to me while I was sitting on the stoop. I didn't know who they where or why they where coming over here. Ut Oh here comes the "Buckets". A bucket is someone that doesn't know you, always putting their 2 cents in or taking 2 cents out no matter what they're just full of shit. Then they said hi what's up. I said what's up. Then they sat down. I was like yo what's up. They said, "are you new here."

I said, "What's up."

They were like yo calm down we just wanted to say what's up. I said, "yeah and."

They were like how did you hurt your leg. I was like. None of your business. They said you're tough. Michael just laughed I think they like that. We just want to say what's up. I took down my guard and told them my version of what happened. I made it sound like I was the baddest person that played street football. They never heard of football on a bike. Then the little one Muhammad said well you can't play that anymore. And then they laughed. Laughed at me. Yo no one laughs at me. Then they walked off. I was piss. Who the hell were they to laugh at me. Sheila came over and I asked her about them. She was so excited that they came over to me. I was like yo Sheila who are they? She started off with Muhammad like she loved him or something. She told me that Muhammad was a nice guy and he was really smart. That everyone likes him. Then she spoke about Michael like she loved him too. She said that Michael was a stuck up kid and that he is in jail more then he is home. I just didn't want to hear about them no more. As we sat on the stoop one of my old friends well not really my friend but Tony, hold up wait a minute here comes the bucket. He came over and said hi Bones did you hear about Tyberius. I said what about him. He said you live here now? I said, yeah what about Tyberius. Then he just walked away. Sheila said who is Tyberius. I didn't answer I just went in the house and left her sitting there. I went in the kitchen and got a knife. Then went upstairs to the bathroom. My sister said what are you doing? I was cutting off my cast. I needed to find out about Tyberius and I couldn't do it with this damn cast on. So it had to go.

I started cutting it off. My mother, sister and brothers where like stop. My mother said, let her do it she would be back in the hospital in no time. I didn't care I needed to go to 203rd St. and see Tyberius. He needs me. And I needed him. If he was here those two guys would not laugh at me. Tyberius would beat them with his dog chain.

I cut the cast off and stood up. It hurted like hell. But I couldn't let my brothers and sister know that. I started walking down the stairs and thank goodness for the rails. Then I went outside and Sheila was still sitting there. She said what did you do? Girl you crazy.

I said, "do you want to come with me somewhere?"

Then we started walking. Sheila let me lean on her when we got to a corner. All the way there Sheila kept asking are you ok. I just kept walking I just had to keep going. When we finally got there I went straight to Tyberius house and knocked on the door. His mother answered the door. I asked is Tyberius home. She looked at me and didn't answer.

I said, I'm Bones I'm one of his friends. She said, come in.

The last time I was in Tyberius house he was having sex with some big head girl. And all I keep hearing is "oh keep going, oh keep going".

Sheila and I sat down. His mother said do you want some kool aid I said no.

Where's Tyberius?

Is he ok?

I mean he's not dead is he?

Then Sheila said, no thank you mam.

I looked at Sheila and calmed down.

Then his mother said, "that the Skulls where up at a restaurant and had a fight with the Crowns and cops came in." and Tyberius got arrested.

I said, "oh so when does he get out of Spofford?

See when he used to go to Spofford he would be in there for about tow to three months. So I felt a sense of relief. She then said he's not at Spofford.

I said, "not in Spofford then where is he?"

He's at Rikers Island.

I said, the island?

Me and Sheila looked at each other like we both couldn't believe it.

Oh no why did they put him there. She said because of his age. Which I never knew how old he was. But damn the Island. That's where murderers, rapists and real bad guys go. Anybody who went there knew then that Tyberius would never be the same. No one was ever the same after Rikers Island. Not even a bad ass like my friend Tyberius. We sat there a little while talking to her about Tyberius and his brother's sons they had with Burnt to Death and her sis, Ruby, and she told me that they moved back to the Bronx. She even told me that Tyberius name came out of the Bible. I knew what a bible was but I never seen one before.

When we left I told her if she every speaks to him or see him tell him I moved to Mangin Ave. and that I miss him. She said she will. We left and went to the park. And there was Tony, he said "one of your legs is darker than the other". I said so what the fuck you care for. He said hey didn't I see you with a cast on your leg just a little while ago. Then he started to talk to Sheila and she liked it. I didn't get that. Why did she like boys. I just didn't get that. He had the nerve to walk us all the way to Farmers Blvd. trying to talk to Sheila and make stupid jokes. That she laughed at. What the fuck is going on with her. Why did she laugh at Tony he's a big headed skinny freak. I knew Tony longer why did he never walk me any place and why he never tried to make me laugh.

Anyway Back to the Hood of Things.

We kept walking and when we got to Farmers Blvd. Tony and Sheila just laugh and laugh. I said come on lets go. By "Tooonnnyyy", Sheila said, he's cute.

I said and you're blind. We left, as we walked up Farmers we stopped and got beef patties. Man this beef patty store was all that there was a Jamaican guy and a Jamaican women there and they made all the food themselves. As we where leaving the beef patty shop some little guys came running over to us. I couldn't help but think it's the "titties". It's go to be the "titties". Darryl and Sam where their names. Darryl was cute he looks like he could have been Sheila's brother. And Sam who looks like he needed a brother I mean he was so poor looking with big clothes on and stuff like that. Both of them looked like they where just little boys I mean they where short yeah but little too. Those little guys started asking us for our names. I thought they were cute. So we gave them our names. They asked if they could walk with us we said ok they were very entertaining. They told jokes and when they smiled they really looked cute. I had to stop walking because of the pain in my leg. By the time we reach the "dock" (Murdock Ave.) they had to go back so then they turned around like the "dock" was the end of the line for them. Man I have to get me some tits (titties) I thought they work wonders. We took the short cut to the house. But the hill on Mayville hurt my leg. I mean It really hurt my leg. I had to stop walking Sheila said are you ok it's your leg right I knew it. It hurts right, do you want me to get your mother, brother what are you ok. I tell you she is funnier then Carol Burnette. Every time she would ask me something her voice changed. I started laughing. She said, what. What's so funny. I said you are why are you changing you voice so much. Then we both start laughing. But my leg wouldn't let up it keeps hurting. Man when we got on the block everyone was out. The Brooks and all their children even Mr. & Mrs. Brooks was out. The Hills with their nine kids which I didn't like any of them especially Paulette. My brothers all three. And some families that I didn't know. Yet, they were playing kick ball or dodge ball what ever and Michael and Mohammad was there playing with them. I just want to sit down. I sat on the stoop and my little sister and Danielle came over to show me their new clap game. Danielle was one of the Brooks children and she was the same age as my sister. She was cute too. With her long pig tails and ashy knees.

Anyway.

They started singing: Down, down baby down by the roller coaster sweet, sweet baby I'll never let you go shimmy, shimmy coco pop shimmy, shimmy pow shimmy, shimmy coco pop shimmy, shimmy freeze.

I watched while they stood there frozen, and of cause I said that Sam moved and my sister laughed. And said, I told you, you moved. I smiled. But the pain in my leg made me stop smiling and rub it. My leg was hurting real bad so I said I'll see you later and went in the house to sit on the couch. My father was home, He said are you ok?

Why did you take the cast off? I said, I'm ok. The cast I didn't need it any more. See my leg did not hurt anymore. See dad I can walk. He just looked at me and went upstairs. I went to my room and crashed. When I woke up. My father was there. He said get dress. I sad my leg is fine now daddy. He said get dress.

I didn't want to go and get another cast on my leg. So I took a shower and got dress. When I went upstairs all my brothers and sister was eating Cheerios. So I sat down and ate too. I was very sad I knew that I didn't want to get a cast on my leg. After breakfast we got in the car which was a job in itself. Everyone wanted the window. They were "calling" the window and no one wanted to sit in the back. My brother Raif got one window and Junior got the other Craig got the back. And I was in the middle. Vanessa like always sat in the front with Mom and Dad.

I was very quiet I just didn't want to get a cast on my leg. And I didn't we went to the Jungle Of Habitat.

Jungle Of Habitat was a big zoo where animals come right up to the car. I couldn't help but to think that my Mother and Father were making up for all the wrong that was or use to go on in the house on my old block. I didn't care it felt good going out. When we got up there Junior was in the back window with Craig. When we got to the gate the man said don't open the window. So of course we did.

The animals were walking all over the place the lions and monkeys oh shit there were a lot of monkeys. I mean there where people out their cars walking right up to the lions. We thought white people are crazy to do that. Man all the black people stayed in their cars and watched.

Then my father said close the window Raif. And when he did a monkey crashed right into it. That was so cool. We all laughed and we talked about that monkey all day long. Inside the park we tried to take a peacocks feather right off its back and man did that bird scream. A security guard came over and took us to our parents. Boy did we laugh. My father even laughed at it too. I don't know what happened but when we moved to the new house we started going places with dad. Like he didn't want to leave us alone in the house anymore. We went places all the time. It seemed like every weekend we would go somewhere. He would take us to Hershey Park and movies oh man did we go to the movies. We use to load up the car and go to 42nd St. and we use to have a choice of who we wanted to go to the movies with. Either mom or dad most of the time we would pick mom. Because she used to see cool movies like Cotton Comes to Harlem and Shaft. She had great choice in movies.

Back to the Hood of Things.

When we came back from the Jungle Of Habitat. Sheila was waiting and boy did we have stories. She didn't even let me finish telling her about my safari, she told me that Darryl and Sam came over. I had to think a while who. Then she said, remember the two boys that was with us when we bought beef patties. I said, oh yeah the munchkins. She laugh and said, yeah. She wanted me to go to Quencer Road with her to meet them. I said, ok. I didn't have to ask could I go I just went. We used to come home and if we had time we played. We started walking to Quencer Rd. and there they where standing there on the corner. They had beer a quart of Olde English I've never drank beer before. And I like it. It was wet and it gave you a funny felling like you could do anything. And it was cheap a quart was like 50 cents I could do that. We sat on the church steps and drank it. The church steps we sat on I didn't know if it was empty or not, but no one came out and no one said anything so we kept drinking.

Anyway.

Even if it did it wasn't Sunday. Then Darryl went somewhere we talk to Sam and drank beer. The beer was nothing compared to what Steve bought back he had a lot of boys with him big boys. At first I seen these boys coming I thought this was a set up. So I got in my stand and put my back against the wall and ball up my fist. And damn my leg I would just have to protect my leg. Ok Gi-Gi lets do this. There was Jim and he was short and stumpy who look like he needed someone to donate him some clothes. I mean he looked like you could stand his pants up and it will walk all by itself.

There was Richie he was a basketball player for his school. Richie looks like a real educated guy. He look like he could hold his own.

And then there was Eric, Sam's brother. Eric was tall skinny and light and cute. Oh my goodness he is cute. Yeah he's a keeper. And they also had beer with them we sat on the church step for hours, drinking beer and talking they where loud and crazy guys. But it was fun. The beer was working its magic, the more I drank the more I talk and the more I wanted to talk to Eric. The guys seem to have the girls they wanted. Richie talk to Sheila and Eric yeah talk to me. I knew I didn't need "titties". Eric was amazing or was it the beer. I didn't know but I liked it. He started to tell me how sexy I was. I never heard such things. I just smile. He said that he thinks that I'm cute and he would like to come over and see me sometime.

Man I thought that he was so cool. Or was it the beer. The more I drank the more I just loved what he was saying. He lick his lips like he just finish eating chicken. And every time he would lick his lips I followed them with my eyes. Man this guy was good. **Or was it the beer.**

I just know that I wanted to taste his lips and I never felt like that before. Damn I never tasted anyone's lips before. And I like it. Then they walked us to my house where I sat on the stoop. Eric sat next to me and then he touch my hand. I touch his hand back. When he touch my hand my body tingled I felt like, I mean I felt like, I felt like a GIRL. I look up and my brother Craig was in the window looking at me. I was like looking back Craig, he wouldn't leave so then I said good night to Eric. When I got in the house I wanted to ask someone what was this I was felling I mean was it the beer or was it Eric or both. But there was no one to talk to. See I'll never tell my mother about Eric. I never told her anything and she never told me anything. I mean one day I got my period and I was so scared I said, mom I'm bleeding and she just went to the store and came back with a box of Kotex and said here use these. I didn't even know what to do with them. I had to get Babs to read the directions on the back of the box. Good thing it was in picture form

I laid down in my room on my big bed and thought of Eric. I grab my pillow and kiss it thinking it was him. Man it had to be the beer. The next day I don't know why I just wanted to see him again. And I didn't have any beer. My brother Junior came to my room and I started telling him about Ole English. I told him how it made me feel and he held on to my ever word. After talking to Junior, I was ready to see Eric and I was so happy that Sheila wanted to go with me there too.

You see she wanted to see Richie. Although Eric was way cuter then Richie but to each his own. Eric lived in a big green house with his adoptive parents. He also had a sister Emily and brother Steve that were adopted also. And Steve was adopted too. Everyone in the house was adopted. I've never seen anyone who was adopted before. They didn't look so different then us.

Oh well **Back to the Hood of Things.**

When we went to his house he came out he had on a tee shirt and jeans and when he saw me he smiled. The tee shirt look too tight for his body, oh shit I can't believe I said that!

He looked real good in that tee shirt. I mean I felt like going to the store and buying him a bunch of tee shirts that were too small. He said he can't come out yet he had to clean the house. Clean the house I tell you he was different, clean the house. I never cleaned the house I just made my bed. Sheila said, we would go home and see you later. Then we went to Richie's house but he wasn't there he had basketball practice. So we went home down Farmers Blvd. And of course we stop off and got beef patties.

Later that day my mother and father wanted to take us to the movies so we went. We went to see the Exorcist and I thought that I wouldn't concentrate on the movie because all I wanted to do was see Eric, but man have you ever seen the Exorcist. My mother had a tendency to sit in the front row and so we did. We also had popcorn, candy and soda. My mom loves to buy us everything we needed in a movie so that we wouldn't bother her or talk. It was strange but everyone sat in the back and we where the only ones sitting in the front then the movie started. She started turning her head around, and throwing up all over the place, and we tried to cover our eyes but my mother wanted us to cover her eyes, man were we screaming. The movie was the scariest movie she ever had us see. Man I mean I was really scared my mother the crazy "movie picker outer". When we left out of there I didn't think abut Eric I just wanted to go home and get under the covers. And that's just what I did. Man that movie had me scared shit. I mean I was in the basement dark damp you could hear all noises in the basement. Man I slept with all the lights on. No joke.

The next day Eric and Richie came over without the munchkins and Eric and I had time to talk to each other. My basement was just right I could let you in and no one would ever know. We laugh and joke about everything then he kissed me. I didn't know how to kiss or what kissing was all about. I don't know if I was good at it or if I'm just a fast learner. But he started rubbing on me and making all this moaning and growing. Then he started touching me in some weird places. It reminded me of Renee and Wade with all this touching and I thought that wow this is cool I'm having sex. Ok I get it. But I really didn't get it. I didn't know what to do or how to feel or what. Richie ended up leaving and going to Sheila's house. So I remember from "Foxy Brown" what to do next so I took down my pants and Eric was so excited. He took off his pants just like in the movies and I thought Cool. I'm Foxy Brown. Then he laid me down on the bed and laid on top of me. It happened so fast. I can't believe it. Wow that was cool I had sex. I think!

Eric was so happy, I was happy too. I didn't know why but whatever. I had sex. When he left I didn't know what to think. I walked him to my basement door and he gave me this look like his eyes were sleepy or something. I just smiled. Then he said, I'll see you tomorrow girlfriend. I sat on my bed and looked around trying to see what happened if I could replay it all over. But it was too fast. I mean not like Foxy Brown at all, no music, no cigarettes after. Oh well I went to sleep, and the next day I told Sheila and she said "cool are you going to do it again". I thought again! You have to do it again! Why? Sheila said, yeah you didn't like it. I thought yeah ok I did. But the truth is I didn't know what the big fuss was all about. I mean you take off your clothes and kiss and lay down and he lay down with you and it's over. I felt nothing. You didn't talk you made no noise. Just lay there.

Sheila said well next time you do it try looking at him it will be better. I said ok well I'll try it. Eric started coming over more and more and we had sex every time he came over and still I didn't get it. I tried everything looking at him, making noises. I even tried to talk to him like in the "Shaft" movies. I tried talking before sex and after sex nothing I still didn't get it. I just didn't get it. One night we were having sex and Eric said that he was stuck. I said "stuck where" he said "in here". I said then get it out. He said let me relax and then it would come out ok. I said does it happen like that you know stuck. He said no this is the first time. Well after that we didn't get stuck no more, but sex still didn't make any sense to me. I wish I had someone to help me I really wanted to know more about sex. Because Eric was so happy. One thing about having sex I notice that my "titties" was getting bigger. After I had sex with Eric all I wanted was beef patties and ice cream. Eric was my boyfriend and I guess I had to keep doing it until I could figure it out.

School started and I was telling everyone that I had a boyfriend and we where having sex. Everyone seemed to be excited until they asked me how was it. I said well fast. Eric was all I thought about. When I got home he was on my mind and I must have been on his cause he was there everyday. On the weekends we would drink beer and eat beef patties. Then we would cross the tracks to go to a party. Going across the track was a real cool thing to do. You had to cross the Long Island Railroad tracks. When a train came don't even be on the track because the wind from the train will almost knock you over. Everyday Eric would say that I was pretty and I couldn't understand why. I started to feel different I don't know what it was. But I was getting over protective of Eric. I was feeling that every girl wanted him. I also started sleeping a lot. I mean a lot. I didn't drink that much beer anymore, but I ate beef patties everyday, sometimes even four or five times a day. My body was changing too. I was getting "titties" and my butt was getting bigger. I know that cause Eric would say your butt is getting big. I also started dressing like a girl. When my mother would take us shopping I would go over to the dress department. Even Sheila would say how nice I looked. I even asked her to do my hair one day. She straightened it and put real pretty curls in it. I don't know what was happening to me but I felt like a girl. For the first time in my life. I even started going back to school and trying to listen when the teacher spoke. Eric was changing my life but Eric and I had problems. You see my mother and father use to fight all the time. I mean really fight, knock down drag out fights. Us kids would get involved. But when they stop fighting they used to have sex. I guess I thought I really had this girl friend thing all figure out. You fight have sex go party all in a week. Life was great.

Well one day I was getting dressed to go to a block party and Cynthia came over. Cynthia was a new girl on the block she had three sisters and they all were so pretty. I didn't like none of them but Cynthia. She seem to look right through me and say just what I wanted her to say. Like when I introduce her and her sisters to Eric. She said that he was fine, and she wish she seen him first.

Anyway, Back to the Hood of Things;

I was in the bathroom and Cynthia said you are going to have a pretty baby. I said what do you mean. She said you're pregnant. You didn't know that you was pregnant? I said no how did you know? She said look at yourself in the mirror.

In my bathroom in the basement I had a bunch of square mirrors. I said how do you see if you're pregnant. She said look Gi-Gi .

I said, I don't see anything. She said look at yourself. So I did. Oh wow I'm pregnant I didn't know that. But serious I didn't see anything.

Ok my complexion was changing, and my nose was getting big, but seriously I didn't see anything.

Anyway.

Eric, James and Richie came to my house to get me and then Sheila. I was walking and thinking does everyone know I'm pregnant. I started walking different. I was taking my time and I keep holding my back. Oh yeah I was acting like I was really tired. But no one cared.

When we started walking across the tracks to go to the party I told Eric that I was pregnant and he was so happy he picked me up and we where happy I guess. I really didn't understand what was going on.

But I went with it. He said, wow if we have a boy name him Erice. I said Erice. Who the hell is that Erice.

He looked at me and said I am, that's my real name they just call me Eric for short. I said oh. Well my real name is Rachel I just call myself Gi-Gi because it was cool.

It was like we just met.

We walk to big Baisely Park and he was just hugging me and was kissing all over me. When we got to the park the music was jammin' and we dance all day the dj was playing a new record Shit Got Damn get off you Ass and Jam. We did the hustle. I really like the hustle. I really like doing the hustle and dancing with Eric and being pregnant I guess. Man the hustle was out of sight. And I really did it real well.

When we left the park, and started walking home. Eric and I kept doing the hustle. I thought man this is the best dance ever. And I really loved the way when you spin how my dress opened up. And then it was the move that Eric did which was called dipping me. I really like that.

I couldn't wait to go home and show my brothers, especially George who was called Junior, he really likes to dance too.

I know together Junior and I can really do good. When we got home the dancing was off.

Raif had thrown records and one of them hit Mrs. James from across the street. From what I heard she really got hurt. But I think her biggest problem is that she told my mother. I mean they said that she didn't even wait until mom got out the car before she told her what Raif did. Big no, no.

Mom lit her ass up. I mean they said that mom cursed her out like she was nothing. And then they said that Michael who at the time loved my brother I think it's because we have the same last name. I don't know but I heard that he beat up Mrs. James son who just got out of jail.

Back to the Hood of Things;

On Monday I went back to school and I was so excited until the Dean asked to speak with me. We had this black Dean of girls. She was always riding me about something. She would say

"Rachel you should go to class one day you're gonna wish you had". Then Rachel if you fight so well why don't you fight the devil who be riding you. And her favorite. If you put effort in you school work like you do in fighting maybe you would pass some classes.

She said Rachel I said what? Are you pregnant? And I was like is there a stamp on my forehead that said hey everyone look at the pregnant girl. And no that bitch didn't just come right out and ask me that. She didn't have any clue.

I said what every sixteen year old would say when the Dean of girls asked her if she's pregnant.

I said, "NO".

She went to grab my shirt to pull it up. She, by this time, saw my pants where too small and I had to have them open and wore a big shirt over it. Most of the time I wore my fathers shirt. He didn't mind.

After school I went home and decided to go to Quencer Rd. and tell Eric that one of the teachers well not just any teacher the Dean of Girls asked if I was pregnant. Eric was in the back of a house that was abandon and we used to hang out there. Really we did more then hang out there it was the new drinking spot.

One day two gang members came over to talk to Eric and the crew. Jim bought them over. There was Sugar Bear who look like he could have been a women. He was all that and a bag of chips. He had long hair like Indian and long eyelashes. Man he was all that. Then there was little Bear who was short and he was real funny he told a lot of jokes. They wanted to tell everyone how good their gang was and that we meaning Eric and them should join. I really think Eric was thinking about it because before you knew it there was a lot of gang members coming over all the time. Then we heard that Sugar Bear went to jail and while he was there some guys gang raped him and Sugar Bear hung himself.

Well you didn't have to tell us anymore about that gang. Eric and the crew said no thank you.

Anyway Back to the Hood of Things;

GI - GI ✒

I walked up to the block and there he was with another girl and I couldn't believe it. I called him and he came so I didn't ask about the girl. He asked me what's up? I said you would never believe this but the Dean asked me am I pregnant. He said what did you say?

I said, "NO!"

I told him with a smile on my face like I did something really cool. But Eric did not smile. I was pregnant. And he didn't smile we were a couple for the whole summer and fall and this was the first time he didn't smile.

Then he said, that he no longer wanted to be my boyfriend that he has another girlfriend. I just looked at him and turned and walked away. I went and got a beef patty went home and thought about it. I mean I really thought about it. What should I do. I was totally out of my element, I know I'll go to his house.

I'll tell his mother, yeah that's it. Yeah tell her that I was pregnant and that Eric no longer wanted to be my boyfriend.

See I seen this in a movie and it worked.

See this girl was pregnant by this guy and she went and told his mother that she was pregnant and the mother told the guy to marry her and they lived happily ever after.

See the guy in the movie went back to the girl because his mother told him to.

But, it didn't work for me. I sat down just like the girl in the movie did and his mother told his brother to go and get him. Eric came in and was mad. I couldn't believe this was happening he talked about going to the Army and getting married and I believed him.

But instead he told me to leave and never come back. This is wrong!

I mean why did it not work for me? I was so piss I stood outside his house and cursed him out. Then he came out and we started fighting.

His mother broke it up and told me to go home. I went home crying and my brother Junior was outside with Felix and he asked me what happened and I told him.

Eric came over I guess to talk to me but instead my brother met him and said, yo man why you hit my sister. Eric was like move out of my way. I want to speak to your sister.

My brother Junior hit him right in the face and they started fighting. I mean all my brothers other then Craig started fighting him. Junior and Raif and their friend Felix.

Wow who knew.

They where in front of the house on the grass. I just went into the kitchen and I was crying. Then I decided to go to Sheila's house, I told her I was pregnant and she said are you drunk?

When I told her that I'm going to tell my mother. She said for me not to tell her but I didn't listen. **To this day I don't know what made me tell my mother. But I wish I didn't.**

Did you ever wish that you could go back in time and change something? Well this was it. It was one of the biggest mistakes of my life.

Anyway Back to the Hood of Things;

I left Sheila's house and went back home and told my mother. She said, go to bed and everything will be alright. I really thought that my mother would go over Eric's house and talk to him but she didn't.

I mean she really didn't even blink. It was like she knew I was pregnant and was cool with it.

The next morning my mother came downstairs and said she made a doctors appointment for me. And we had to go tomorrow. I thought ok.

You know go to the doctors, and every thing will be ok. I tell you the truth I really didn't know what was going on. I mean here is my mother the meanest women I ever knew.

I mean she really doesn't like me but she seemed to be ok with this.

Man I should get pregnant more often.

We went to the hospital early that morning. I mean it was real early. My father drove us. I didn't say anything in the car and all my mother said was George you will have to pick her up ok. He said ok.

We went to an office like, in the hospital, and a lady well a nurse came up to me.

She took me in this room and put something some metal thing put up you. Then I got dress it was over in minutes. Like sex. Then the nurse went over to my mother and said she is three months pregnant. My mother said she is. Then the two of them started talking back and forth like I wasn't there. Then the nurse started asking me if I wanted to use birth control pills, I U D or get my tubes tied. I didn't know what she was talking about. My mother said an I U D would be fine. I wanted to ask what is a I U D? I mean really.

The nurse said are you sure? You can say if you don't' want an I U D. I was like this bitch didn't know anything about my mother. I looked at her then looked at my mother and I knew not to disagree with her so I said I'm sure. Then the next thing I knew I was laying in a room with my legs spread open. I looked at the doctor and said, I want my baby please don't take my baby away.

The next thing I woke up and I was in a room full of women. It looks like a waiting room for the damned. They where taking things out of peoples draws and stealing kotex. One of the women said are you ok. I said, what happened?

She said you had an abortion.

I didn't even know what that was.

I was the youngest girl there and I didn't understand what had happened. And no one would say anything to me. A nurse came over to me and said wash up and put on your clothes your parents will be here in a while.

I asked her where my baby is.

She said get dress and wait for you parents. So I did. It seems like forever. I mean I felt like I stood outside for hours. Then my father came and picked me up. And he said you see what trouble you got into. See.

I just look out the window of the car and cried. I wanted my baby back. Why did they take my baby and where did they put my baby. But I knew not to ask my father. So I just sat in the car and looked out the window and cried.

When we got home I looked at my mother and she had this look of happiness in her eyes.

Like yeah, bitch I got rid of your baby.

I looked back at her and I just pushed passed her and went to my room. Then she had the nerve to come to my room and say, don't get those sheets messed up. Or I'll make you sleep in them forever without washing them.

The feeling that I felt for her that day I can not put in words. I mean I could but, she's my mother.

The next day I went looking for Eric but he didn't want to talk to me. It was like he knew. Everybody on Quencer Rd didn't want me to come back on the block no more.

I mean that's what they said. I just didn't understand. Where was I suppose to go.

What was I suppose to do?

So I went to my house and sat on the grass with Sheila and got drunk. And that was Gi-Gi.

CHAPTER 4

Uasia

I had an I U D in me that meant, I can't get pregnant any more. Everyday I wanted my baby. There was not a day going by that I didn't think about my baby.

Sheila decided that she didn't want to go to Quencer Rd. no more. So Sheila and I went to Baisley Park to hear some new DJ at night we where sitting on the bench and HY-Kim came over he was a peace god. A peace god was a 5% nation of Islam. I mean Hy-Kim was like a giant. It was like when he walk the ground would go boom, boom I mean he had presence. He was not like tall giant. He was a giant of a man. A mean man. He was with guys who names where Shahim, supreme and names like that. They asked us our names and I said Gi-Gi and Sheila said Sheila.

They asked us what school we went to. I said Jackson and Sheila said Jamaica.

My outfit was a pair of jeans and Marshmallow shoes with a mock neck. It was the funniest thing but the peace god had on the same thing other than the marshmallow shoes. They had on little Abners instead, or hushpuppies. I heard about these peace gods but really didn't know anything about them, just that they where popping up every where.

I knew that they were not real serious peace god because they didn't have on gators.. All I knew is that they where springing up all over Queens. And that they where all black and that they had a style of their own. Oh yeah and that I was a savage in the pursuit of happiness. It was the winter time the pee coat was a must for a peace god. Trust me if you weren't a peace god you still wanted to wear a pee coat. They where the shit. Peace gods had short cut hair that they called the "ceaser". And they spoke funny. Like peace god and earth. Like power equality all see equality. And the most popular was "My word is Bond" and "bond is life". Shit like that.

Anyway, back to the Hood of Things.

Hy-Kim and me hookup right off the back. Like the next day he came over and was like you are my earth. I was like what. Oh yeah when a peace god said that you are his earth, that's like someone else saying be my girlfriend. I said ok to Hy-Kim. I knew that I needed someone to be with. After Eric I was really lonely. Lonely the first emotion I learned after Eric. Lonely.

Laying in the dark with no one in my bed lonely. He was so big and I mean it was like he lifted weights or something. And you know he really did lift weights!

He lived in a house off Baisley Blvd. this was the south side of Queens. He lived with his father. His mother had died years ago. I don't know how, I didn't ask. I just knew I wasn't lonely anymore. So he and his father just stayed together in a three bedroom house. Hy-Kim had the basement. And it had a washer and a dryer in it. I never seen anybody but Sheila with a washer and a dryer in their house. Hy-Kim was more like the father then his own father was. His father was even shorter then Hy-Kim. And very quite. He didn't call Hy-Kim, Hy-Kim he called him Raymond his government name. Hy-Kim answered to it. He showed me around the house. And said that he never really go upstairs but if I wanted to I could. I asked him do he have any other brothers or sisters. He said yeah he had two sisters, they were married and he had three nephews. He also was the baby of the family. And when he said that he smiled and shit he had dimples. All of his friends I mean peace gods call him Big Hy-Kim. I stayed over his house a lot. I mean he never lock the basement door. When he did he would put the key under a mat so I could come in and out.

When I use to come home from being with him, the door would be locked to my house, I'd climb through the window, if the window was locked well, let's just say, it was up to my brothers to let me in.

They would stand by the window and laugh. I mean they use to laugh real loud, but I knew that they would open the door and if they didn't I didn't care. I just went to Sheila's house. She always let me in. You see ever since my mother had that doctor and nurse take my baby from me, I just didn't want to be around her.

Everyday I use to leave home and go to Hy-Kim's house where I learned how to turn a one dollar bill into a twenty dollar bill. See Hy-Kim and his crew use to have a hole bunch of funny money, and they were good at passing it off. He taught me every thing he knew. I mean I learned how to cut the bills so that I wouldn't cause a crease, that's bad because if a clerk would feel the bill, if she felt a crease you're busted game over. I learned how to wash money so that the ink would be a little worn out so it would look more natural. I even learned how to stack it so that when you count it you couldn't tell one from another. When I was good at it he took me to Pathmark in some white people's neighborhood and took me shopping.

Boy I couldn't believe that I was not nervous or anything and it was easy we had a lot of food and we would get it for twenty seven dollars. The cashier would think it was one hundred and sixty dollars. Then we would get in a cab and go to his house and split the food. Hy-Kim was so proud of me.

He told all his friends that I was a natural, that I was real cool. Then he took me home. I really enjoyed that because I use to bring food home. At home I hated my mother I tried not to speak to her. She took my baby away from me and I hated her for that.

I would think that my baby was walking around looking for me and didn't know where I was. I know I keep talking about my baby. But I really miss my baby. Can you understand that?

Anyway Back to the Hood of Things;

When I brought food home my mother use to ask me where did you get the food from. I just looked at her and walk away. She knew not to touch me so she didn't. Being with Hy-Kim gave me a sense of strength. I mean really I felt powerful and I could kick anyone's ass and if I couldn't I knew that Hy-Kim could and would.

I use to put the food in the frig and my brothers and sister was like yeah sis went shopping. After a while I use to go to see Hy-Kim my littler sister wanted to come with me. I really didn't want to take her.

We had to walk pretty far and I really didn't want to bring her, but there was something about her. I didn't want her to ever look down at me. I knew that she was just so "syked" about me and my new money. So like always I would break down and say ok.

If she came she just use to pee on herself every time. I use to beg her not to pee on herself but there she would pee on herself. But I didn't care Hy-Kim had a washer and dryer at his house so we used to wash her clothes and she used to look so cute sitting there waiting for her clothes to dry.

Anyway.

My little sister and I used to go over all the time. I really enjoyed being with Hy-Kim we didn't have sex that much and that was alright with me. He was faster than Eric. And I still didn't get it.

We did something better we stole things. Clothes and food. He taught me how to walk in a store say in Manhattan and walk out with a watch, hat, jacket, pants, shoes, stockings and yes something to eat. I loved it.

Figured that if you can lie you can boost and boy we all know I can lie.

I loved the new clothes that I was getting. Especially that it was free. He wanted me to learn how to play C-Lo, and for those who don't know this is shooting dice, but it was getting real cold outside so he said he'll wait till summer.

One snowy day Hy-Kim told me to go home and stay there that he would see me later. He didn't understand why I hated to go home. I just use to tell him I hated my mother. He didn't get it.

"Stay in the house I mean it", Hy-Kim said.

See I had a tendency of going boosting by myself and he didn't like that. He said, How about if you get busted boosting and I didn't know what happened. I'll feel real fucked up.

So I never went boosting by myself I always took someone with me. Plus boosting is more fun if you have someone to share it with.

So I went home. My mother, brothers and sister was there waiting to see Captain Kirk and the Enterprise. So I went down stairs took a shower and put on one of my new night gowns and bathrobe that I got boosting and went upstairs to watch it with them. I was sitting there thinking that man it's been a long time since I've been here.

I looked at my sister, who was laying on the floor, my brother Raif who was stretched out across the wrap around couch, and Craig who just opened the door to his room where he could see the TV. Damn it's been a long time since I've been here.

Anyway.

I was sitting on the couch. When Sheila walked in and went right upstairs. I don't think she even saw me. I guess she never expect to see me in the living room. When she came down my brother Junior was with her. I remember thinking boy did he get tall. My brothers been around. He started to do graffiti all over the place his tag was Fuel. He used to tag with a guy from the Bronx named Big John. They tag on trains and even on the wall of the garage in my back yard. Big John and Fuel tag a picture of the skyline. It was wonderful. I never really knew that my brother was so talented. But he was not only that boy Fuel he had a rep. I mean the tag crews knew him well.

Back to the Hood of Things;

I said, hey where you guys going. They said to a party at the Sunrise. That was located on Baisley and Farmers a new club that Hy-Kim and his boys used to go to. At the Sunrise you could be strapped and no one would even say anything. I knew the guy at the door. And you know what I wanted to go there man how about if he tells big Hy-Kim. But what the hell.

So I got up and my sister said I thought you would stay in the house with us today. I was just about to change my mind and stay then I looked at my mother. And I knew I didn't want to stay with her. See when I saw her there was this felling that used to come over me. I can't explain it but I always removed myself from where ever she was. It was like something would move me away from her. I don't know if I'm saying this right. ***But Anyway.***

I went and put on some long johns, my favorite jeans, my new silk shirt that I stole from Macy's, a sweat shirt, my pea coat and gloves and my "kicks", and went with them.

The Sunshine club wasn't even opened. There was snow on the ground and man was it cold. But outside this guy told us where there was a party in Hollis. See that's how you got to a party someone would tell you and with a smile you would go. Sometime there's a party and sometime there's not.

Anyway.

We went to Hollis the party was in a church and man it look like everyone was there. It was a crowd outside and a crowd inside, you can hear it. And the beat was on. Then we saw something, the door opened we ran over to push our way in. That's another thing we did. If you didn't have to pay, why pay. Then a shot was fired I don't really know how many it happened so fast. Sheila and I went to the side of the church where other people where too. They heard the shots also. Man we were pissed, we really wanted to go to the party. The beat was on! As we coward in one spot an old black man with a gun came and told everyone to leave. It was cold and snow was on the ground. When he came I mean, it looked like something from the "Twilight Zone". I mean all you really saw was the shadow. I admit I was spooked, but man did the other people, that were there in the cut, run. It was icy outside and I had on new clothes.

Anyway.

Sheila and I don't run for anything and we didn't.

I mean I'm Uasia. I was from Mangin Ave shit I wasn't running. Plus if I fall. Man I was not running. Then by time we were halfway at the gate to leave. Tony blocked it. Tony was a light skinned brother who was always into some shit. I mean if he wasn't fighting someone or in the middle of some shit. I mean no one really knew him. Everyone just heard of him. It was just my luck that he was there. If we knew that he was there I don't think anyone would have been there. Word he was trouble. He had a gun and was aiming it. So Sheila and I moved out of the way. If they wanted to shoot each other then, so be it. Who was I to stop them? I like a good shoot out. When we turned around to see where that crazy old man was. The crazy man with the gun was aiming right at Tony and then both start shooting.

Come on, Sheila and I was out of the way. That's why, damn Sheila went down and I got piss. She was saying I'm shot, I'm shot. I said you bastard you shot my cousin man what the fuck you can't shoot. Then I felt what I thought was a cigarette burning me. It felt like it.

It really didn't hurt I just noticed it. I thought nothing of it. Then Tony and the crazy old man left. I turned around and Sheila was on the ground. I don't know how long all of this went on it seemed like seconds.

The cops came and then the ambulance came and took Sheila away.

I was standing there I couldn't believe that Sheila was shot. The cops started asking me what happened. But I was no snitch. I just said I don't know someone started shooting. That's all I knew.

I was also looking for my brother. The funny thing about it, the party, the beat keep going on.

I was just standing there frozen wondering what I should say to get me out of this mess. I knew everybody would blame me. And damn where's my brother.

When a cop came over to me and said young lady are you ok.

I said, "no my cousin got shot."

He said, "are you shot?"

I said, "no."

He then said, "open your coat".

I was like yo I'm not strapped.

I thought, oh shit he thinks I shot Sheila. I said look I didn't shoot no one.

He said, "Miss open up you coat please".

The please had it so I did and blood was everywhere. My brother fuel came over at that time and look at me and I looked at him. But it was the way he looked at me. Then I looked at the cop, the way they looked at me made me look down at all the blood that was on the ground. My blood covered the snow. And I thought I'm gonna die.

The cop said, "Where are you shot?"

I said, "I don't know."

My brother just looked at me. Like he was trying to memorize my face. Like this is the end. The ambulance came and put me in the back. Fuel came with me he keep saying oh shit, he shot my sister. By time I got to the hospital my jacket, sweat shirt and new silk blouse were off. And I had a blanket over me. No one said anything in the ambulance. I was just quiet, or I was just looking at my brother and I had blanked everything out. I was thinking damn I wish I spent more time with him. I thought about my sister and her smile. Raif with his big feet and chicken legs. Craig wiggling his ears. But most of all I thought about my baby that I would never see.

I got to the hospital and Sheila was there she said what happened?

I said, "I got shot."

A nurse with a big ass needle came towards me and said this may hurt a little.

I said, "bitch no it won't because you're not sticking me with that."

I don't like needles and you are not sticking that no where!

They held me down and the needle didn't hurt they just put it through the same hole that the bullet traveled through, but what ever was in the needle did, and I screamed.

I said, "Am I going to die."

Man did it feel like I was on fire. It really burned. The nurse said that it was medicine to clean out the after effect from the bullet. I didn't care what it was that shit burned. It really hurt.. And that's when my mother and father walk in.

My mother said, "You won't die bitch only the good die young."

I thought now what kind of shit was that to say. Here I am laying down on this slab with a bullet in my stomach and all she can say is the good die young. Man I wanted her to leave. Then my father came and he look at me like it was my fault. Can someone at least act like they care about me. While I was focusing on my parents the doctor managed to put an IV in my arm and then I was asleep.

When I woke up I was in a room that was all white, I thought yeah I'm dead I must have been good. Finally no mother.

See I told everyone it was not my fault. But I was not dead; I was just in the hospital. I still had an IV in my arm and I felt my stomach and it was all bandaged up. My sister's voice is what I heard first and she was smiling. Then I saw my father in the chair next to me. He must have been there all night. Then my mother with my brothers came in. They had the Sunday paper with them.

My sister said, "See mom she woke up."

My mother said, to my father here George I bought you something to eat and the paper.

My sister said, "I'm glad your not dead."

They surrounded my bed and asked me all kinds of questions like did it hurt, can I see. I told them it didn't hurt and no you can't see.

I said, "where's Sheila?"

My brother Fuel said that she was home they let her go that same night. I said really. He said she got shot in the ass, and we laughed. The doctor came in he said we can't remove the bullet from her stomach. It was a 22 and they were afraid to move it. My mother said so she is going to have the bullet in her? The doctor said that it will travel and hopefully that when it stops we would be able to remove it but not at this time. It's too close to her stomach, and if we go in and touch it, that it's a possibility that it might damage her more.

So there I was in the hospital with a bullet in me. I was so cool. I'm the first girl on my block that has a bullet in her. I'm probably the first girl in my school with a bullet in her. Damn maybe in the whole world. I don't know how long I was in there but it felt like forever. They just kept me there, and everyone came up. The police were the first that came. And they had a story that we where trying to rob the church.

Whatever.

Hy-Kim and the peace gods came up there. They were telling me about boosting and how they miss me. They also had some weed and asked me if I would like some. I never had weed before but I said ok. And I puffed it. Man I choked and some of the gods started laughing. Hy-Kim said let's go to the bathroom. So he helped me out of the bed and went into the bathroom with them we were laughing and joking but the weed made me sick, so I went back to bed. I don't think it mix well with the medicine the doctors where giving me. So Hy-Kim helped me out up on my feet and took me back to the bed. I felt really tired and told Hy-Kim that I was going to get some z's so he said peace and left or what the gods like to say he traveled.

Then the next visit was someone I totally didn't expect Eric. He had on this big black hat and well if I had to say so myself, he really looked good. I think the black hat with his skin color really worked for him. He was telling me that everyone knew that Sheila and I was shot. But let him tell it and it was all my fault. I couldn't understand that. I got shot damn. I did not have a gun. I was with Sheila and my brother so how was this my fault? I told him it was not my fault but if you want to think that, then so what if it was?

Why are you here then? Boy you should have seen the look on his face. Then he said I was just telling you what I heard.

I said so, now you told me see yah.

He said, so is your peace god coming up here to see you?

I knew that Hy-Kim would be there any minute and that's on my mind I felt like yeah fuck you Eric. But before Mr. Eric would leave he had to tell me about his new girlfriend and that they where having a baby.

A baby I said, you are not even looking for the baby that I had. Eric do me a favor and get the fuck out of here you jackass. That worked. I couldn't believe that he was having a baby and my baby was out there somewhere and he didn't even bother looking for it. What a jackass. Then the pigs came up to visit me again, asking me all kinds of questions like why where you there? Are you Uasia? Did you have a gun? Do you know who was also shooting?

Man what the fuck. How did you know I was Uasia? They then tried to flex their muscle and say answer the question. I mean we were just going to a party, and none of us had a gun, that crazy bastard just shot us.

How did you know my name was Uasia?

Then they left without even answering my question. How did they know who I was? When it was time to go home boy was I happy.

I went in and it was winter and came out it was almost spring.

Damn I really got shot. The hospital had the nerve to give my parents the p-coat and the blouse I was wearing but not the hoody. When I got in the car my mother said you should have been a boy. My father just looked at me. I got in the car and I had the same window like always. When I looked out the window it reminded me of my baby. I don't know why but I thought about it all the time I was in the hospital. When we got home I went straight to my room and laid down. I must have went to sleep because I heard my father say are you hungry yet Rachel. I said in a minute. I went to the bathroom and took a shower.

I had to be real careful because you could touch the bullet under my skin. And if I touch it the wrong way it would hurt. Then I put on my bathrobe that Sheila gave me. It was terry cloth, and it was like putting on a towel, and I went upstairs. For the first time in a long time we were all at the table eating and daddy cooked.

As I looked around the table, I saw Fuel who when he saw me looking at him he winked. Then I looked at Craig who just kept eating. Then I looked at Raif he was tall. And I remember thinking damn he got even taller. Then Vanessa just as cute as ever in her own way. I knew that this will never happen again we will not be all at this table like this again. I just had that feeling. So I enjoyed it. Oh yeah we had a dog. Topaz a German Shepard. As soon as I got better I went to see Hy-Kim. I was wondering where was he and why I haven't seen him. So I went over there. I looked for the key under their rug, but there was no key, so I knocked. A girl answered the door. A light skin girl with thick black hair. She had on a big robe and slippers and she had a baby with her. I said where's Hy-Kim?

She said, "In jail for boosting."

Then I looked at the baby who was in a box on the side of the bed. I remember thinking why is this baby in a box. I looked at her and the baby and said "is that Hy-Kim's baby?"

She said, "Yes."

Then I asked her do you know when he would be back. NO. Damn. I asked her are you ok she said I don't have any money. I said what you mean no money.

She said, "That she came over one night and Hy-Kim told her and the baby to stay here he would be back. The next thing she heard is that he was in jail.

I said so how long has he been gone she said about two weeks. I said did you talk to his father he would help you.

She said he is helping me with food and stuff. But, Hy-kim had a lot of money down here and I can't find it. I look at her and smiled she really think that I will show her where Hy-kim hides his money. I said, well good luck finding it. Then I asked her do you know who I am.

She said yes you are Uasia.

I said did Hy-Kim tell you about me.

She said that you had got shot and if you ever come over here for me to let you in.

That's all I wanted to know. Then I bounced.

With Hy-kim gone it was no fun boosting by yourself so I went back to school. I tried to go to all my classes and I tried to listen to the teacher. But, the first time I failed a test it was over. I started hanging out in the stair case by the lunch room playing c-lo and smoking weed and of course o'e. One day we were playing c-lo, and I was wiping the floor with those ass holes, and the pigs came and we ran. But, the only place to run is the lunchroom and when we busted in there and sat down, the pigs just came over and picked us up. I mean it was like I had a sign on me that said hey I was one of them who was playing and smoking on the steps. They had cuffed us put us in the guidance counselors office. They had us in the office one at a time. I had to really do some thinking cause before you know it, it would be my turn. O shit here we go. Think, Think come on Uasia get yourself out of this one. Then I saw her, my "mark". It was the principal asst. she was a little white lady, who would swear that everyone liked her. But, in reality we were just using her. She was funny coming from her lily white neighborhood to help us poor black kids do right. I laugh every time I saw her talking to one of us. Because I knew she was just a mark. I said could you get someone here so I can get these hand-cuffs off to get some water. She said there is no one here yet.

I asked her in my most convincing voice could you get these handcuffs off me so that I can get some water. I pleaded with her saying I am so scared and I really am thirsty. She left and came right back with a key. She took the handcuffs off and I was out. I walked right out the door and down Murdock Avenue. Every time I saw a cop car I ducked.

Don't let me hear a siren man I was scared. I mean I just came back to school and I got a bullet in my stomach. I was not going to jail. But, I guess it wouldn't be that bad I would see Hy-Kim. I went home and went right upstairs to where my mother and father was in bed.

I said daddy they arrested me in school and put handcuffs on me see. I showed him my arms where the handcuffs where. I mean they had them on tight. Boy was daddy angry. He got dressed and we where in the wagon and the next thing we were at school. My daddy was pissed and I loved it. He walked right in the principals office and said you handcuffed my daughter are you fucking crazy.

The principal came and tried to tell my father all these things that I've done. Like I was the ring leader of the school.

Like I was the only one in the school playing c-lo come on this is one of the badest schools in Queens, if not the badest.

The news media used to live in front of the school waiting for a story.

And believe me they got one every day.....

Andrew Jackson High School. Everyone knew it. My daddy didn't care what they said he was just pissed. I said daddy they threw me against the wall. That was all she wrote.

He was heated. I mean he started pointing his finger and whitey started running around trying to justify handcuffing a black girl. Then they took daddy to the stairway to show him where I was and that I was playing c-lo.

Daddy said, "I don't give a fuck what she done."

If you put your hands on my daughter again I will sue you. Then they said, ok Rachel go back to class. But daddy said no she is off today. I was so glad my dad was the man again.

The next day my guidance consoler called me to her room. She said that she has an appointment for me at Fashion Institute.

Fashion Institute what the hell is that!

She said, "a school in Manhattan for the arts."

I thought yeah they just want me out because my father was going to kick their ass yesterday.

She said, "that I have a gift and I should use it."

I said, "What gift."

She said, "You are always well dressed" and I told her that "I like to draw clothes". I said, why did I tell you that?

She said a long time ago. I thought damn she remember that. Then I sized her up. I looked in her eyes and she was serious. She really think I could design fashion. I went home and told my father about what she said. My father said, do I know where this school is. I showed him the pamphlet that she gave me. He said are you going?

I said, "yeah."

My mother on the other hand didn't say anything. And that was cool with me.

So the next day I woke up real early and took out my freshly press Lee's and I went into Manhattan and to the Fashion Institute.

The school was different from Andrew Jackson there was no grass or trees there. And in the hallways there wasn't a bunch of kids hanging out and there was no c'lo.

I did find a guy in the hallway and asked him "where is the audition at".

He said, "I'll show you follow me". No just point to it, But he showed me. I was in a room with other kids my age and a lady asked me my name, but she had some kind of accent like French or something like that.

I said my name is Rachel Brown. I was sent here by Andrew Jackson High.

She said, "ah yes Rachel what a pretty name. Then she gave me a script and ask me to memorize it and be papered to act it out. But my reading was not that good. There was another girl sitting next to me a white girl. I asked her the words and she helped me read it. I mean she didn't make fun of me, she just helped me. So I memorized it and then they called my name. And the white girl said good luck. I was like good luck? What the fuck does that mean.

I went inside and there where four people there. And they where all white, three men and a women. They were sitting at this table. Then another guy came in and started speaking to me and I said, my lines and they said thank you we will be in touch. Well that was it. Thank you we will be in touch.

White people and the way they speak.

Anyway.

I just went back home but not before I stopped at a little store in Manhattan and did some shopping you know what I mean. No sense of wasting the day.

I told my brothers where I was and what happen. I'm telling you we don't have these things happen ever day.

The next day the guidance counselor called me to her room and said that they thought I was good but my grades where too bad for their school. I said cool I didn't want to go to that stupid school anyway.

But you know really I would have like to be there. I don't know what it was about, but it would have been nice. So I went back to hanging out, this time I went to the back and sat on the bleachers. Yeah we found a new place to play c-lo and I couldn't wait to tell Hy-Kim about it I was getting really good at it. Making about 20 dollars a day.

The next day wouldn't you know it, that same guidance coun-selor she called me to the office again. Like what's up with her is she going to call me in her office every day. She said, that the guy teacher wanted to meet me that there was some guy there that was looking for runners.

I said, "runners."

Like I did something wrong and the cops were chasing me, runners.

She said "you're not in trouble but yeah," "runners".

She said you do know how to run don't you.

I smiled and said do I know how to run. Then she said do you have your sneakers with you. I said, no but I still can run. I mean if cops are chasing you, you don't have time to say hey officer wait, let me put on my sneakers.

She took me to the back of the school where there was a lot of girls there. And two white men.

They said who is this?

I said, "I'm Uasia".

They said well you can't run without sneaker.

I said listen I can beat these girls running with or without my Adidas. The guidance counselor said, this is the girl I was telling you about. Let's just see her run.

They said, ok let's see.

I look at these girls with their shorts on and matching sneakers and said boy are they going to look stupid in my dust.

You have to run the fifty yard dash lets see how fast you can do it.

I said, "cool."

We had a line we had to start at, and the white men had these watches on a string and whistles in their hands. And my guidance counselor stood next to them. She was looking at me like you better run. They blew the whistle and I was off. I ran that in 5.4 seconds with shoes. And beat all the girls. But my grades kept me from getting that too. I told the guidance counselor thanks but I don't want to do this again. I was tired of her trying to show me off to her white friends. I was tired of her white friends saying that they didn't want me. I was tired of her calling me in her office, and for her not to say shit to me again. Leave me alone. And that was the end of doing something good in school.

I went back to pulling smoke alarms and sticking teachers in the elevator. Man sticking teachers in the elevator was real fun. To hear the teachers screaming for help made my day, not to mention that the fire department had to be the ones to let them out. No school that day. Well almost no school. The principal started to get up on it. And just stop school until the teachers could be released then he would make us go back to class. Then one day I was walking to the ladies room. I use to always go to my Junior Psychology class. I really like that teacher. He was a little white man who looked like he was high on something. He use to tell us about some guy that use to ring a bell and his dog would go crazy thinking it was getting something to eat. I really like that class. He use to make us draw pictures on paper then tell us what kind of people we where. He would see my paper and say you are a very dishonest person. Man he was real smart. I was sitting in class and I started feeling sick. I asked him could I go to the bathroom. He gave me a pass and I started walking down the hall when I felt pain in my side. My side was hurting me real bad and my left leg couldn't move. My leg locked up, I couldn't even bend it. It was almost the same pain I had when I broke my leg. But it was five times worse. I grab hold of this kid and told him to call the ambulance. He ran and got the principal. Then they called the ambulance.

I asked the principal what was wrong with me.

He said, just relax the ambulance is on their way. When the ambulance came I heard the principal say "it seems that the bullet got stuck in the joint of her leg".

They said a bullet did she get shot.

The principal said yes sometime in January.

They said "we'll call her parents and have them meet us at Queens County Hospital". Then they put me on a stretcher and the principal held my hand until I went in the ambulance. She really looked like she cared I guess or maybe she was glad I was gone. I went right into the operating room and with one cut the bullet was out. I was so glad. Only my father and brother Fuel came up to get me. School was over for me I missed so many days due to me getting shot and staying in the hospital. But they promoted me anyway. My brother Fuel will be attending the same school as me when it started up again, and I really didn't want him to. This was my school and I know he would tell on me. The things I do in the school no one knew but the people I wanted to know. Well, no sense of worrying about that now, it was hanging out time.

So I started hanging out with other girls who's boyfriends where peace gods. Like Sandy, her boyfriend's name was Malik. Mary and Nana were her friends. We use to go to parties everyday. I knew all the clubs in Queens. We used to go to this club on Jamaica Avenue. Until they shot Buddy.

He was a thirteen year old guy who had like five fine brothers and he was the youngest. He used to have us laughing when we would see him. He just was one of the funniest guys you ever seen. But someone must have not thought he was that funny so they killed him. I was like three people behind him when the shot went out. Everyone looked around and there was Buddy laying against the wall. I was like damn now we can't go to the club. I was also piss that blood got on my white silk mock neck. You can't get that out you know.

Then hard times came against me and the girls. We use to smoke so much weed that we didn't have enough money to smoke weed and go to parties. So we decided to snatch bags. But that was such a waste of time.

Sometimes you can snatch a bag and get twenty dollars and some food stamps. But then it was the time when you would snatch a bag and get a dollar and a token. I mean after snatching a bag then running three or four blocks to get away from the shouting women, all you get is a dollar and a token. I called a meeting with my girls. We needed to come up with a better way of making money.

I said, we would meet on the cool out that night and talk about our ideas. So I started home and stopped at Little Giants grocery store. I wanted something to eat.

As I was in the aisles there was this girl, she was stuffing snacks down her pants. We caught each others eye and I said you need help?

She said, yeah if you want to.

So I didn't stuff snacks down my pants, I just picked up a bunch of steaks, snacks and walked right out the front door. Like everyone else did.

I met up with her outside.

She was like oh shit that was bold.

I said I'm Uasia

She said I'm "Angel Fire".

I checked her out up and down. She had on Lee's ok. She had on a Lee jacket ok. And she had on Adidas ok. She was also real pretty. She looked like she had some Puerto Rican in her, with her wavy hair. I was like where do you live. She said around.

I said yeah well Angel Fire I live right up the block would you like to come and cook these steaks.

She said ok.

We went to my house where we meet up with my brother. Mr. Wiggle Ears himself Craig. I took the steaks and went in the house and put them in the oven. Then I came back outside and I was too late. Craig already was showing her his roach collection. He had real roaches running around in a jar, and Angel Fire was cool with it. She said "hey your brother is real crazy look at these roaches". If you shake the jar they all look like they are dead then they start to crawl again.

I was like man she's a keeper. So I told her about my crew and I wanted her to meet them. So we ate the steaks and went to the cool out.

I stood there while the girls checked her out, I think they really dig her name Angel Fire. We started discussing how we where going to make money. Angel Fire said why don't we rob a vick.

We laughed and said we tried that we snatch pocket books already and the money wasn't right.

She said, not that kind of vick, Guys. They got money and they always want to spend it on us. We where like ok Angel Fire where you from. We can't rob guys we're only girls. I said well wait a minute We can get one guy outside, wait and it's five of us shit. Why can't we rob them. It was me, Angelfire, Nana, Mary & Sandy. But how do we rob them without them knowing that's what we're doing.

So we sat there on the cool out making up a plan on the Vicks.

A vick has to have nice shoes (they wouldn't want to run in them).

A vick can't have hems hanging form his pants (that means they don't' take care of himself).

A vick has to have good teeth.

A vick has to be a vick, we have to check him out and know who is with him. Yeah. That's a big one we don't want to be caught off guard.

And the biggest one is that you do not dig the vick remember we are here to make money.

That's it.

We waited til Friday and went vick hunting. We started close to home like the I Can Club which was right around the corner.

We went in and did our hunting. Then I notice Angel Fire talking to this guy. He was all into her then she looked at me and I knew vick time. So we all went outside and waited. She bought him out and we said ok this is vick time give us the money. He was like you bitches then we started to jump him five girls on one guy yeah buddy.

Then we took the money and went right back into the club. And man he didn't even follow us. That night we scored two vicks and seventy five dollars. And we didn't even break a nail. The next day we expanded to Baisely to the Sunshine Club. The Sunshine club was cool I mean really cool there was so much meat there that when we finish vicking on guys in less then five minutes we were vicking another. We like got one hundred and forty dollars. And still no broken nails.

Then on Monday Sheila came over and said that they are giving out jobs at Man Power for me to come with her to get a job. I was like cool. So we went and sure nuff I got a job working Monday thru Friday 8am-12pm for a bunch of Jewish Ladies they had a Thrift store and I never been in one before. My job was to look through clothes that people did not want anymore and pull out the really bad clothes and put them in a basket for 5 dollars an hour.

Ok I can do that. I did it for Sheila. I think she knew what I was doing. And was trying to save me. From me.

But working for these ladies was more then just a job. I mean they opened my eyes to a lot more. They had on something that I have never seen before, diamonds and a lot of gold. I mean these ladies hair was done and they all smelled so good. They seem to like me. They use to tell me about places to shop for underwear. I was like underwear.

They said yes if you are going to wear diamonds you should always have on sexy underwear. I never heard anyone talk like that before. They would tell me to go to Macys and go to the un-derwear department and buy you something pretty like silk. So I did and did and did. I had so many pretty underwear that Sheila wanted some. I use to take my underwear to the cleaners to get them washed and dried and ironed. Man there was nothing like beating up a vick with silk underwear on.

Walking up to a vick and knowing that he was going to pay for your underwear was so "deaf".

You know those clothes that they where getting to sell was not that bad. One day there was a Japanese coat made of silk it was green with a beautiful peacock on the back. I never seen something so pretty before. So I asked one of the ladies can I buy this, and they said "yes, for a quarter".

I put that on and it was nice, then I would hit a vick and all he could remember is the peacock.

We were so good at this that we started to take our little show on the road. I mean everyone in Queens knew about some girls robbing guys for money and giving them a hell of a beat down. We took it to Brooklyn and just like Queens there was a vick. But Brooklyn vicks didn't have that much money and so we took it to Manhattan, bingo. Manhattan boys was all she wrote. You talking about money we made almost three hundred dollars from one guy outside of this bar. Then we heard about a twenty four hour spot we went there and we made about one-hundred and fifty dollars. The only thing about vicking Manhattan boys is that we had a long way to get home. But it was worth it. We decided if we need a lot of money we would go to Manhattan. But we really wanted to stay in Queens. We went to rob some guy on the south side and he screamed and ran. Man I almost wet my pants. Then one day Nana picked out this vick but by this time we were all over the street news. We told Nana not to pick anyone today that we would go to Manhattan but no she wouldn't listen. The vick knocked her the fuck out with one blow. He caught us by surprise but when I pull out the 38 just like everyone else he was vick-timized. He also got an ass whipping.

It was blood all over the place and damn he bled on my new "dogs"(my shoes).We had to take a cab home to drop off Nana. Man I knew it was the worst cab ride she ever had we laughed at her all the way home. That was our summer, vicks and work. Work and vicks. And later that summer Angel Fire got busted for something. She was such a secretive person that you never knew what she was up to. I never knew what she spent her money on, or where she lived. Sandy spent her money on Malik. Nana spent her money on her mother and little brother. Mary spent her money on records, and I bought silk underwear and Adidas. But we never knew what Angel Fire spent her money on. And you know we never asked her. That was just her way.

Back to the Hood of things..

I was at the bus stop going to my job and there she was with a wool coat and sweater looking like she was in a snow storm. It was July. I know New York is cold but damn.

She said, that she had to go to court and that she may not get out for a while.

I said damn Angel why you didn't tell us. She didn't answer.

I Said you want me to go with you.

She said no but wait for me to get home.

I said, I'm not going anywhere. She said, I know.

We got on the bus and it was like I was saying good bye to a real close friend. I got off the bus before her and gave her fifty dollars that I had in my pocket. She smiled and winked and that was that.

That night we sat on the cool out waiting for Angel Fire but she didn't come by 10pm so we knew that she was not coming. Now we could have stayed home that day or just chilled with a quart and on the cool out but not us.

We wanted to party. That night we went to a club on Jamaica Avenue it was a quiet club but we heard a lot of gods went there. So we did too. Well really Sandy picked it out I think she was looking for Malik, and wouldn't you know it he was there. He asked us what where we doing there.

I just looked at him, and kept walking to the bar. Truly the only person that would answer him was Sandy.

She said, we just wanted to hang out.

He said , ok, but he didn't want her to dance with anyone and don't rob anyone here. See Malik and Sandy's relationship was funny. He was supposed to be a real peace god, and a real peace god didn't have a girlfriend that robs vicks. So he use to keep it a secret that he was with Sandy, and she didn't even mine. I was like fuck that she should go to the peace gods when Malik was around with a pork chop in one hand and the book of life in the other.

We where at the bar I ordered some ol'e and was chilling when this guy came over. He had a Gucci hat on with a matching raincoat and umbrella all in black and brown. He squeezed between me and Mary. Boy did he smell good, usually the guys smelled like sweat but not him.

He has a good smell like he put on Tabu or something. He looked at me and said, "What is your name?"

I said, Uasia."

He said, "I heard of that name before you live in Jamaica?"

I said, "yeah why."

He didn't answer.

He said, "Could I buy you a drink, then he pulled out all this money and the top bill was a twenty.

I said, "No thanks I have ol' e". I smiled and when he smiled it was like the room stopped and there was no one in the room but him, his smile and me. I don't know if he was talking I just keep looking at his smile. The brother had perfect teeth and I think he knew that. I had to look around because I really was wondering if he was a setup.

Sandy said, "I would like a drink."

He looked at her and started to ask what she wanted and I said she doesn't want anything. See we used to rob guys like that all they had to do is pull out the money again and it would be over.

The look on Sandy and Mary's face they wanted him to be a vick. Then his friend came over and whispered something in his ear and then he looked at me and smiled, but his eyes where like inviting. I don't know but I was opened. Then I looked at him and he walked away with his friend. Sandy said, "Damn Uasia why didn't you get him, he had all that money, what's happening?"

I said, "I just didn't feel right about that."

He felt like a setup.

She said, "yeah now he's gone."

I looked around and she was right he was gone. I don't know about this but every time the door will open at the club I was looking for him. I said look girls I'm ready to go and we shouldn't be hanging out anyway with Angel Fire in jail. We where like yeah. So we left. That is after Malik met Sandy at the corner to get his sneak kiss. What a sucker. We walked down the Ave. and we kept trying to see why Sandy was with him. I mean we would hit vicks and she would spend her money on Malik that didn't have enough respect for her to introduce her to his peace god friends. She really hated when we spoke about Malik like that. But what was up. We went to the bus stop as we where waiting for the #3 to take us home. A gold and white Seville came over to where we were standing. This was a bus stop, usually when a car came up in the bus terminal there's a hit on someone. I reach for my guy which was a 38 pearl handle special that I took off some guy last time we were on the Ave.

The car stopped and he got out.

I said, "yo you shouldn't do that!" I was going to wet you up. He smiled and said would you like a ride home. I just looked at him and I was getting ready to say hell no but, before I could say anything Sandy, Mary and Nana got in the car. I stood there looking at them and they said get in our feet hurt. I just stood there. I knew we would definitely rob them and I just didn't want to. I mean four thugs and two well dressed guys this is definitely a set up. Then I looked at him and he said, " I promise not to hurt you." I felt like Diana Ross in Lady Sings the Blues and he was Billy D. Williams.

He said, "I really love your coat."
I said, "Yeah."
He said, "Is that silk?"
I said, "Yeah."
He said, "So you don't want to get in?"
I said, "what's up with you and your boy?"

He said, "I really want to get to know you and I was on my way home and I noticed you standing in the terminal.

I said, "you notice me."

He said, "well I notice your coat."

Sandy said, "come on let's go, get in the fucking car already."

He said, "well your friends really want to go."

I said, "yes they do."

He said, "but if you don't want to then I wont." What you say?

I say well I just, it's ok. So I got in. While we were driving home I sat in the back really all four of us did.

Sandy said, "so you guys go around picking up girls you don't know".

He said, "I don't know you?"

What you say?

He said, 'well you are women and I am man so I do know you. Mary said wow that was real sexy. I looked up at him in the mirror and he was looking right at me. Yeah he was sexy but I really didn't know what was up with him. I knew that the cops where "up on us". For some reason I thought this was a set up. We dropped Sandy off first, then Nana and then Mary. Which left me alone with Billy D and his friend.

I said, "hey what is you name?"

He said, "Everlasting Lord Kendu God Allah and that his friends name is Darryl that they been friends for a long time ever since they where kids. I was like well Everlasting Lord Kendu God Allah do they call you anything for short.

He said Kendu.

But you can call me Lord Kendu.

I was like alright Lord Kendu, so you guys riding around huh.

He said, "Looking for you" then he looked at me in the mirror again. I was thinking what is this guys angle. I mean is this guy real. I kept my hand on my gun. Fuck that I was out numbered, but I was not out of bullets. When we finally got to my house I tried to open the door but it was locked, Lord Kendu got out and opened my door for me and reached out his hand. I took it I felt like a queen. He walked me to my door then we sat on the stoop. We talked about everything. I mean outside of the car he was really, really sexy. He was looking behind me. I said what are you looking at.

He said is that your brother?

I was like oh shit not the boys. I turned around and it was Craig wiggling his ears.

I smiled and said that's my brother Craig act like you don't see him. But listen I would love to continue this talk but he would just get worse. So I'm going inside.

Then he asked could he see me tomorrow and I said that would be ok if you could remember where I live.

He said, I would never forget where you live at I will be here tomorrow. Ok.

I said, "ok."

Then I went inside and watched them drive away. I couldn't believe it. Wow what a guy. I went into my room and thought wow what a guy. I found myself thinking about him Lord Kendu and that was a bad thing. I knew that I would rob him one day and I didn't need to think about him any more, he was a vick. There is no way you should be thinking about a vick. So I blocked it out and went to sleep.

The next morning I heard someone calling my name and I didn't recognize the voice I laid there real still. Then I heard a guy say she would wake up with the sound of my voice. I put my hand on my gun. I thought oh shit the cops. Then I heard my sister laugh. If my sister is with him he must be ok. So I rolled over on my back and opened my eyes. All I saw was his smile. I jumped up and said what are you doing here.

He said, I told you I will see you tomorrow. Who let you in and I looked at my sister and said ok. But yo you shouldn't come in my room without asking me first. Don't do that again.

He said, "after today you won't care if I'm in your room or not. Matter of fact you would wish I was in your room."

I was like yo Lord Kendu. I was going to curse him out then he looked at me like he was looking in my soul. I said nothing. I told him to wait for me over there. I pointed to my living room area. I had a ripped up couch but it was mine and he went and sat on it. I took a shower and put on my white lace silk under wear. I looked at myself in the mirror and was like yeah that looks good.I put on my favorite jeans and a blue mock neck and my white on white high top kicks. When I came out the bathroom he was not there so I went up stairs. When I went upstairs he was on the couch with my three brothers. Who were asking him about his watch. I just stood in the living room and looked at them. I couldn't get a handle on this guy. He fit with them. He didn't look like they where bothering him and they really look like they liked him. My brothers would put guys through it. That's why I wouldn't bring any guys after big Hy-Kim home.

One day I made a mistake and bought this guy home, he sat on my stoop. I wanted him to wait for me and when I came back to see him there was no one on the stoop. I looked for him and found him at the bus stop on Farmers Blvd. I was like why you left? He said your brothers said they would kill me if I didn't, so that was that.

Anyway Back to the Hood of Things.

Then my mother came downstairs and I wanted to take him and run out of the house but, before I could he said hello my name is Kendu. The brother stood up and held out his hand like he wanted to shake it. My mother took his hand and said hello. Then she said I'm Mrs. Brown and who are you here with.

He said, "I've come to take your daughter Uasia to breakfast is that ok with you". My mother said you have a nice smile. She said so tell me again what are you doing here? He said I'm here to take Uasia out for breakfast is that ok with you. My mother smiled and said no one ever asked me is it ok to be with my daughter before so yes it's ok with me.

I thought please I didn't need her permission to go anywhere. Fuck that. He looked at me and said you look nice are you ready to go.

I said, you look nice too. He had on black pants with snake skin shoes, a white shirt with a tie and a pee coat on and a black hat. He looked back at my brothers and said peace. I remember thinking man does he like his hat. I said, "I'm ready." We walked outside and there was a black and gray Maverick sitting in the front of the house. I asked where is the Seville.

He smiled and said that was my mans car. He opened the door for me and I sat in then he closed the door. Man was that getting old. I could open and close the door for myself. He got in and we were off. We ended up in Crown Heights at this little restaurant. Where I ordered pancakes. He ordered the same. He sat across from me staring at me. I was thinking what's taking these pancakes so long. What are you staring at?

He smiled and said you. You're the only one sitting here.

I said, why you are staring at me.

He said, because you are so beautiful.

What you think I'm beautiful?

He said, yeah don't you?

No one every asked me that before so I couldn't think of an answer so I didn't answer.

He asked me when is my birthday.

I said, March when is yours.

He said, March.

I was like this guy is lying. I said what day in March are you born he said the 3rd.

I said I was born on the 13th on a Friday.

He said, really I never dated a girl who was born on Friday the 13th. Then the pancakes came and saved me from this bullshit conversation. He took a napkin and put it on his lap. So I took a napkin and put it on my lap, and that fucking napkin fell. I don't know what piss me off more the fucking napkin falling or that I was so uncomfortable of a guy like that thinking I was beautiful or being in a restaurant.

I said, this is bullshit and moved the pancakes out of my way and said what's your angle what the fuck do you want and why the fuck do you want me and I said it loud. You got me here in this fucking restaurant with these fucking people, so what they could see a hoodlum. Do you think I need you to give me breakfast cause I don't. Then I stood up and said fuck this and left. I was heated. I just wanted to leave this bullshit world and go back to my own world.

I was standing outside trying to figure which car to steal so I could go home. Well ok I was waiting for him to come after me. See I saw that in a movie. And he did.

He said, "I'm sorry if I made you uncomfortable".

I said, "fuck that."

What the fuck do you want?

He said, "you. I want you Uasia."

"Why did I rob someone in your family or something. Are you hard up for someone or did you make a bet. What is your angle man." Then he smiled. I said, "and another thing stop smiling what the fuck is up with you smiling all the fucking time. I mean what are you so fucking happy about."

He said, why don't you smile at all. I smile because my life is good. Why don't you smile?

I said, "because there's nothin' to smile about". And another thing stop opening up the door for me I know how to get out the car what the fuck do you think I can't get out the car all by myself!

He said, " ok want me to drive you home or do you want to come with me."

Did you hear me, I said.

He said, " I couldn't help but to hear you, you talk so loud and when you use the word fuck you got even louder." So do you want to come with me or not.

I said, "as long as you don't take me anywhere where I have to use a fucking napkin."

He said, "ok."

I opened my own door and got in the car. He was real quiet and I felt bad. Maybe I shouldn't have cursed him out like that. I mean look at him the brothers fine. Damn now I didn't get to eat and you know I'm hungry. Man why didn't I just shut the fuck up. Then we went to a park where there was water and ducks. I never went to this place before. It was kind of nice. We got out and walked toward the water. It was beautiful there were people jogging and there were kids laughing and playing. He sat on the grass and so did I. We started talking about what school he went to. He went to an all boys school in Brooklyn where he hates it. Brooklyn High.

I said, "I couldn't go to an all girls school."

He said, "why you don't like to be around girls."

I said, "yeah when and only when I want to."

He said, "so you are the oldest in your family?

I said, yes and are you the oldest in your family?

He said, "no I'm the baby."

I looked at him and smiled he said what. I said I can see you are the baby. How many are there in your family?

He said, "me and my brother."

Really your mother don't like kids? He laughed a little and said I guess after me they couldn't do better. Then we laughed. I said well after me my family tried to correct a mistake so they had four more.

He said, "you're not a mistake".

Then this man started telling me such wonderful things. Like the black man is god and that I am the earth. He started telling me about he is the original man. And about an arm, leg, leg arm and head. He even started telling me about the earth being or rotation 360 degrees. And about cipher. All this talk about earth and rotation made me want a joint. But I didn't tell him that I just kept listening while this great mouth moved. Then he said with your black skin you have not been diluted by the devil. That instead of going around taking life I should be creating life. He started telling me that I flow like the ocean and that I am put on this earth for one thing to give birth. All this talk about ocean and flow made me want ol'e but again I didn't tell him that. There was something about the way his mouth would move, and when he thought that he really made a point his eyebrows would go up, and when he was really serious how he would get this cress in the middle of his face. I was just looking at him, he was perfect. Maybe he was god. I didn't care what he was all I knew is that he was with me. He kept talking on how beautiful I was and that there is so much to me that I didn't even know. And that he would love to teach me. I don't know but the word teach sounded a little too much like school, and we all know how much I like school. I was like anyway are you going to talk all day. He looked at me with this crooked smile.

I said, "what?"

Then he said do you want some ice cream?

I said yeah that would be cool.

He said you're not going to curse me out and walk away again.

I said no.

Promise?

I said, "What?"

Promise me you won't .

Ok I promise now can we get some ice cream please. As we walked to the car I said you can open the door for me if you like but don't do it if it looks like I'm going to do it.

He said, "ok."

Promise?

Then we smiled and he said I promise. We got ice cream and when they gave me my ice cream Lord Kendu said no napkins please, and then we went to his house. He lived in Rockaway apartments. Where all the rich people did. There was a security guard at the gate and he had to show a ID to get in, then he parked the car. Each car had a parking spot. All I thought is damn I got to bring my girls over here. This place smells like money. Lord Kendu must have known what I was thinking.

He said, "oh yeah please don't ever rob this place."

I said, "What?"

You know please don't rob this place.

I just smiled.

He said, "look, you do smile."

We walked into the apartment building and it was so clean. No junkies, hoes or the smell of burnt feet. It even had an elevator. By time we got to his floor we were laughing. Lord Kendu made me feel so nice. Is nice a felling?

Anyway.

I really started to like him. When the elevator door opened up he took my hand and lead me to his apartment door. He used a key to get in. I never even had a key to our house the door was always opened. The only person that was home was his brother Mark and he was in his little room playing a guitar. But I couldn't hear it. Lord Kendu said this is my brother Mark. Mark this is Uasia.

He said, hi and I just nod my head.

I asked him what are you doing.

He said, I write songs.

I said, for school and stuff.

He said, no for music and stuff.

I said how that's going for you.

He just smiled and said it's ok. I make a living. I thought not a good one he's living in an apartment and his guitar doesn't even have a sound. Mark didn't look anything like Lord Kendu, I mean Mark was skinny and had a long face. And Lord Kendu was perfect. I thought maybe they have different fathers. Lord Kendu took me to his room. Where there was a bed, chair and a big mirror. I looked at the mirror and said yeah I could see him looking at himself all day in the mirror. I took the chair and sat down.

He said, would you like something to drink?

I said yeah you got any o'e?

He said, No! No one in my family drinks.

I said, "well I don't want any juice who the fuck drinks juice".

He said, why do you curse so much?

I said, I don't curse so much. So he sat on the bed. I looked at him and said now what?

He said, "do you like kids?"

I said "What?"

He said "Do you like kids?"

I said "What kind of question is that to ask."

He said, "I don't know I just want to know more about you."

I said number one yes I like kids. Number two "I even got a kid. I never seen it my mother took me to the hospital and I was three months pregnant and I had an abortion. So they took the baby and when I asked where is my baby no one would tell me."

He said, "you had and abortion?"

I said, "yeah."

He said "and you think your baby is alive and they took it."

I said, "yeah."

He said "do you know what an abortion is?"

I said, "yeah that's when you have a baby and they take it from you and give it to someone else. Of course I know what an abortion is. I mean what the fuck you think I'm stupid." He had this weird look on his face.

I said, what god did I say something wrong? You don't want to be with a girl that has a baby.

He said, you was three months and you think that your baby was three months.

I said, yeah he was.

Then he said I'll be right back. I thought this guy is weird. When he comes back I'm going to ask him to take me home. When he came back he had a book in his hand and I said oh no you don't want me to read do you.

He said, no. I'm going to read something to you.

I said, look Lord Kendu just take me home. The thrill is gone. Then he started to read like he didn't even hear me. An abortion is when you take an undeveloped fetus and dispose of it. I didn't know what he was saying and undeveloped fetus what, what are you talking about. Look Lord Kendu it was real but I really want to leave now. I stood up and he said come here, so I did I sat next to him on the bed and looked at the book. It had all these words in it and I said what. Then he turned to some pictures of naked women that where pregnant. It was three of them one was a little pregnant then another was a little bit bigger, then the other one was really pregnant.

I said, so what am I looking at. Look I don't know how you get your thrills but you're bugging if you think I'm going to sit here while you show me pictures. I don't know what kind of freak you are but I'm out.

He said, how do I tell you this?

I said tell me what?

Then he pointed to the naked lady that was a little bit pregnant and said do you see this?

I said yeah what?

He said, she is in her first trimester.

I said what? Listen Lord Kendu I really want to go. Then he said something that caught my ear. She is three months pregnant. Do you see the baby this is how little it is when you are three months pregnant. I felt like someone just messed up this movie and put a real fucked up movie in, that I didn't pay for and didn't want to see. Then he said, when you take a baby away from it's mother when she is three months pregnant. The baby dies that is an abortion.

I felt like someone pushed me in the pool and I couldn't swim. I was drowning.

I said, are you telling me that my baby is dead. What kind of person are you! Are you here to hurt my feelings. Well it's working. I should really fuck you up.

He said, your baby is dead it never had a chance. That's what an abortion is about. No one told you.

I felt like crying but, I didn't want him to see. Then he closed the book and took me by the hand. I looked down at the book on the floor and then looked up at him. And when our eyes met I just started crying. My baby is dead and an abortion is when they kill your baby. How could anyone kill a baby? Why didn't they tell me? No one asked me if I wanted them to kill my baby. What the fuck is going on. Then he hugged me and I started fighting him. How can a perfect man say these things to me? Then we cried together. As we were crying the bedroom door opened up and there was his mother. I looked at her and she looked at me. Lord Kendu didn't even look at her. He just wiped the tears from my eyes and said hi mom this is Uasia.

She said, hi what's going on kids?

Then Lord Kendu looked at me and continued to wipe the tears from my eyes, and said we were just reading something mom. Nothing is going on.

She said, why are you crying my son?

I thought my son who talks like that. Damn this is a great time for some ol'e.

He said, it was a really good book mom. Then she came in and picked up the book, and said this is my nursing book. What was in there that made you cry?

I said, they kill babies. Abortion.

She said, well I don't think you kids should be reading this book again.

Lord Kendu said, well we won't. Then he looked at me and smiled and I smiled too. Are you ok, he asked?

I said yeah, but I wasn't I couldn't stop thinking about my baby. My dead baby. I wanted to blow up the hospital and kill everyone in it, except the babies.

He said, let me take you home ok.

I said, ok.

When we got in the car he said are you sure that you're ok. I really didn't mean to make you cry.

I said yeah but that's ok I'll be alright. The car ride was quiet and "BLS" was playing but Lord Kendu and I didn't say a word. I guess we both were thinking about the baby. When we got to the front of my house I looked at him and said, I'm tired, I'm going to bed.

He said, let me walk you.

I said, ok.

We sat on the stoop and Sheila came over and I said Lord Kendu this is Sheila. Sheila this is Lord Kendu. She smiled and said hi. He said, peace.

Sheila sat down with us and we were both quiet and I think she felt funny like we didn't want her around, but that was not it. I just learned that the baby that I thought was alive was not, and the biggest heart break is no one told me. Lord Kendu properly was thinking that he was the one who told me that my baby was dead. It was a funny feeling to have while sitting on that stoop. I didn't know whether or not I wanted to tell Sheila my best friend so I decided not to. We sat on the stoop and then my brothers and sister came over and before you knew it the stoop was jumping. My brother Fuel had just stole a radio and we had the music jamming.

They start joking on Lord Kendu and then he said, you don't have to call me Lord Kendu just Kendu would be fine. I looked at him and said all this time I was calling you Lord Kendu and you mean I could have just said Kendu well damn thanks a lot. Everyone started to laugh. Felix my brother Fuel's friend started telling us all these funny stories and we laughed before we knew it. It was time for Kendu to go home. I wanted to ask him to spend the night with me, but I didn't.

I don't know but it was something special about him, maybe because he was god, or maybe because we cried together.

I said, see you tomorrow.

He said, yeah then my brother Craig said that we won't be here, that we are going to see our Uncle Sal who is my fathers youngest brother.

I said why?

Craig said, that he bought a big house so daddy is taking us there.

Kendu said, well I'll see you when you come back.

I said, peace.

He turned and smiled and said Peace Earth. That moment just that two words coming from him made me feel a little better, peace earth.

The next day for sure we went to my Uncle Sal's house. He bought a brownstone right across the street from Prospect Park in Brooklyn. I mean there were two bathrooms on every floor and the living room was so big you could put my house in it. Uncle Sal was known for the women he married they where all weird like him. I mean they all like that funny music I think it was called Jazz. My uncle was a jazz player, and the biggest pot head you ever meet.

Anyway, Back to the Hood of Things

His wife was into reading palms and shit like that, and my mother and her were friends. Then they came over to me and said "Rachel we know that you have an I U D in you but, that doesn't mean you can have sex a lot". I looked and them and thought wow bitch. I looked at my mother and she smiled like she just let the water out the damn. I could have punched her in her face. Then she started to read my palm and she said that I was bad luck and that my mother should take me to see a Priest.

I said, fuck that.

My mother looked like it was a confirmation to every thing that she thought. That I was the devils child. We went to leave and my fathers car was on four center blocks. Someone stole his tires. I was like yeah maybe that's my fault. Good for them. When we finally got home I ran in my room and took a shower.

When I came out my mother was there.

She said, so you see because you were born on Friday the thirteenth you are bad luck. You see someone other then me said that. I just looked at her wishing she would disappear. I stood there closing my eyes and opening them. But every time I opened them she was still here. I even tried wiggling my nose but that didn't work either. Then she said that she didn't want anyone down here. But I think she could see in my eyes that I didn't give a fuck what she said. Then she asked me where I was getting all these clothes. She was looking at my silk underwear and my new yellow blouse that I was going to wear today. But I didn't answer her. She said, well since you got so much money maybe you should get your own place. I just looked at her and didn't answer her. Then my little sister came down and said mommy I'm ready. I looked at her and it was like a stand off. She took my underwear in her hand and threw them down on the floor. I didn't even budge I just looked her right in the eye. I know she was thinking what I was thinking. But I didn't move she no longer matter. She killed my baby. She was a zero.

When she left I took those underwear and threw them in the garbage. Then I picked out another brand new pair. I don't know why but I needed to go to the Hospital. So that's what I did I went to that hospital and said I need to see a doctor. They got me a doctor and I told him that I have an I U D in me and I wanted it out. Just like that it was gone. On my way home I thought yeah I'm gonna have nine babies, and I wont tell my mother about them. I well never let her meet them. I wanted nine boys so we will all get together and whip her ass.

The next day Kendu came over. I knew because you can hear the dog bark. Then my brother calling for the dog. Then the screen door slam. Then nothing. Then Kendu came down stairs and said that the dog bit him. I was like word. Then he showed, his ripped up pants was on my bed. Then he said he will see me tomorrow. Then we can go to dinner.

I said, dinner.

He said yeah and I want you in a dress and take those braids out of your hair let me see your hair.

I said, where are you going?

He said, home my leg hurt.

I said, peace.

I ran to Sheila's house like someone was chasing me. I opened her door and said hi we're going out to dinner tomorrow and I need to fix my hair. Kendu wants to take me to dinner, Sheila I need your help.

I said, Sheila could you make my hair look like yours, huh Sheila.

She said, yeah I could do that. Where are you going out to dinner?

Kendu said it's a surprise I don't want you to straighten it.

How about corn rolling it? I said well he wants to see my hair. The princess style would be nice, right. The princess is when you straighten your hair and put curls all over it. Black like me was this style that the curls would be under the over, you know. It looks like you have on a hat. Sheila said wow, Kendu has a real nice smile. I was like yeah he does, doesn't he. I felt like peeing all around Kendu to mark my territory. I think Sheila knew it.

I said, Sheila is he fine or is he fine.

She said, yeah where did you meet him?

I told her I was at the club with Sandy you know Malik's ol lady and NaNa, you know black Nana and Mary.

She said, how did you meet him?

I said, we were looking for a vick and there he was. Before we could take him off he was gone. Then he and his friend gave us a ride and that was all she wrote.

She said, yeah all she wrote. Well did you sleep with him.

I said, no he didn't wow, I'll do that tomorrow, then we laughed.

Sheila said, yeah tomorrow.

The next day I looked at my mother. I wanted to ask her about the baby but I didn't. I told her that I am going to dinner with Kendu, and showed her the dress I was going to wear and she said, "well you're going to need a pocket book".

I said, for what?

She said, every girl that wears a dress has a pocket book. Where are you going to dinner.

I said, I didn't know that.

She said, then you are going to need a pocket book. Then she gave me twenty dollars and said bring me back my change. I was like I got money. But then I thought fuck it take her money. I took the twenty dollars, and I wish I could have went back in time I would have never taken that twenty dollar bill. It was another one of those times you wish you could take back. But there were no "backsies".

I went over to Sheila's house but she wasn't there. She went with her mother to her sisters house. So I went over Sandy's house and told her about me going out with Kendu.

She said, did you want me to come with you to find a good pocket book.

She said, that at J C Penny's Nassau there are a lot of pocket books. I'll go with you hey, let's get Nana and Mary.

I said, cool.

But Mary couldn't come she had to watch her little brother. So it was just Sandy, Nana and I. I was so hip, I mean school was going to start back Monday and I was going to tell everyone about this good looking fuck that I was going to bring him up there. When we got there they said they where going to look at clothes and I said cool I can get a bag. I went to the store in the mall. I mean they had a lot of pocket books. So they went upstairs and I went to the hand bag department. I saw a bag in patent leather. It will match my shoes that I stole from the Ave. It was a clutch bag. So I bought the bag and it was ten dollars so I told the lady to put the change in the bag. Then the bitch stapled it so tight. I was like what did you do that for.

She said, I have to that's store policy. I mean she stapled it and had a ticket on it.

Whatever.

Then I left. I was on the elevator when I saw Nana, I went over and asked her are you ready?

She said, no Sandy's in the dressing room trying something.

I said, well hurry up I got a date.

Oh shit I can't believe I said that and I don't think Nana could either she looked at me, and we smiled at each other.

She said, I'll get Sandy.

I said, ok but don't tell her I said that word DATE. Then I went over to the jelly bean collection where a little white boy about ten was.

I said, what are you doing?

He said, if you guess how many jelly beans are in the jar you can win some money.

I said, well I know how many jelly beans are in there two hundred.

He said how do you know that?

I said, because it's always two hundred. So he put down two hundred and so did I.

I said, hey maybe we'll split it. He looked up at me and said shake on it. So we did.

Then Nana said we're ready. As we were going down the escalator Nana and Sandy were behind me. They had two big bags full of clothes.

I said, you guys sure did a lot of shopping. They just smiled. I was like yeah but no one stapled their bags just mine. I went through the door first. When I started to walk further a little white lady with black hair pushed me and I said bitch and punched her and down she went. I heard "freeze don't move".

I turned around and there where three big white cops in plain clothes with guns drawn.

I said, yo she pushed me.

Then one put me against the wall and another one went over to her and helped her up.

I said, yo that bitch pushed me ask her!

Then the cop said, she's a cop.

I said, yo I didn't know that. They hand cuffed me and put me in a car. I looked back and she was holding her face and there was a lot of blood. We didn't drive far. Then he put me in a room. I was like yo I didn't know that bitch was a cop. Come on! This is bullshit! One of the cops sat down and started with the questions. Where do you live?

I said, why?

He said, I'll ask the questions.

I said, Queens.

How old are you?

I said, why?

He said, do you have I D.

He said, did you pay for this bag?

I said the receipt is on the fucking bag or can you see.

He said, you have a smart mouth.

Whatever.

Then another cop came in and said that her friend both say she asked them to come.

I said, I did.

I needed a pocket book.

They said, well now you will go to jail. I said, this is bull shit.

I said, for what?

But they didn't tell me. I couldn't believe this I should have never went to Nassau County no blacks really like going there. It was like you had a sign on you saying "I'm not from here just arrest me now".

Anyway, Back to the Hood of Things:

They took me to Nassau County State Prison. Man prison now what. I stripped and had to wash my hair, it was the rule wash your hair. I looked around at the CO's and thought I could take them. You had to wash your hair with some bull shit to make sure you don't have lice in your hair or any kind of bugs. Like they couldn't see if you had bugs. This is bull shit. Then they checked all my holes to make sure I didn't have anything in them. I mean ears, nose, mouth and yes ass hole. I wish I had to take a shit when they looked in my ass. Then I laughed to myself. One of the CO's said you think this is funny. I just looked at that bitch.

I said, what am I in here for?

They said, you would see when you go to court.

Then they gave me a flowered dress and said welcome to Prison.

Whatever.

I remember thinking what a date this is. They sent me to cell 67. That was my new name 67. What an ugly number 67. I mean what is 67 then I thought damn it added up to 13 here we go with the bad luck, devil shit. I had to stay in the cell for the first day. I couldn't even make a call. But I new the system so I just waited for a CO to come by and I said my parents don't know I'm in here can I at least call them please.

She said, I have to ask and when she came back, my cell door crack and she walked me to the phone.

She said you have twenty minutes make it good. So I called Sheila.

When she answered it my brother and Kendu were in her house.

I said, yo Sheila I'm in jail.

She said, in jail! Then she started asking me all these questions which I didn't have the answers for. I had to cut her off.

I said, tell Kendu that I can't go to dinner with him.

She said, Uasia is in jail and she can't go to dinner with you.

She said, he left.

Yo you mean he was there why you didn't let me speak to him.

I said, so what did he say?

She said, nothing he just left. Fuck him. I heard my brother Junior say ask her when will she come home.

I said, my court date is Thursday so I'll probably be home Thursday.

She said, what happened?

Then I told her.

She said, well I never liked Sandy and Nana anyway. I said, yeah well I got to go now I'll see you later but if not stay cool. Then I hung up. I went back to my cell.

It had a cot, gray wool blanket, sink and a toilet. It sucked big time. But my cell was cool. I was right next to the TV. Underneath the TV was a table and bench and a deck of cards.

The next day they bought me breakfast, my cell was still locked until the doctor cleared me, or should I say since I didn't have lice. When a girl bought my food I looked at it and made a decision no to eat it. I just drank the milk. Yeah that's what I'll do I just keep drinking the juices and milk. I should be alright. I thought they would spit in my food. But the drinks were always closed. Plus I didn't want to depend on anyone to make my food for me. I couldn't wait for this cell to open and I could see what's up and who would be my vick. I was peeing on the toilet that everyone could see you pee and I heard a guys voice I thought that I was hearing things. I mean you could really hear guys talking in the toilet, boy did I laugh. Then my cell door opened I walked out and took a look around. My cell was not far from the front. There were three cells before you got to mine. Then there was a shower for one. I said man this is fucked up. Then I went pass the phone and down stairs there were girls about fifteen of them dancing and singing some playing cards and some watching TV. I didn't want to be a part of this so I left and went back upstairs to my cell. I decided to make the best of a bad situation. At least it wasn't the Island, and it wasn't crowded. But I couldn't help wondering how people could get use to being in a cage. I don't think I would ever get use to it. Maybe Maybe I will accept it but never get used to it. On my way back to my cell there was a little short white girl in cell 66. I walked in her cell and said what are you doing here.

She said, that her boyfriend and his friends came up with an idea to rob a bank. I was like oh shit, I wanted to rob a bank but never could get enough guys. I sat down I had to hear this. I mean she was at least 5 feet tall and looked like she weigh about 100 lbs. Damn I had to hear this.

She said, it was a good idea she was to drive the get away car. It was her mothers, and it was easy to get it. her mom let's her drive it all the time. Her boyfriend and her where going out since at least 2nd grade and they wanted to get married. But they didn't have any money so they came up with this plain. Her boyfriends father works in the bank they were robbing so they knew that he wouldn't tell on them.

I said did you have on masked?

She said, no we didn't think no one would say anything, I mean everyone knew us.

I was like this bitch is bad.

So they drove up to the front of the bank and they went in she said, like in seconds they came out with money but in no bags.

I said, what they do just snatch.

She said, yeah I guess it was not such a good idea.

You think?

I said, go on.

She said, as they where driving away she was so busy looking at the money that she didn't see a little boy crossing the street.

I said, what?

She said, a little boy was crossing the street.

I said, and?

She ran him over and kept going she couldn't stop. So she drove the car up to her house and they got out.

She said, that her boyfriend said maybe we shouldn't have

done that.

She said, that she remember thinking "yeah, it's a great time to tell me now".

She said, the cops came right up to her house.

I said, why didn't you leave New York?

She said, all we wanted to do was get married. Now she is facing life.

I said, Damn 66 life.

What happened to your boyfriend?

She said, she didn't know the last time she saw him was in court. That she don't speak to any of the girls and she doesn't come out of her cell if she can help it.

I said, why?

She said, because she killed a kid.

I said, well it was an accident.

She said they don't care these girls just look for something to start trouble about. You are new here.

Yeah.

66 said, the girls were talking about you being some big shot in Jamaica.

Yeah so.

She said, well they are throwing your shoes around. I turned around and walked outside her cell. I saw my "Fred Barns" in the hallway. I picked them up and put them in my cell. Then I walked to see who the fuck did this. I had to walk to the last cell and there where about four girls in one cell. One of them had her face in the toilet with a pillow covering her. I stood there just long enough to add the dramatics to the seen.

Then I said, hi I'm 67. The girls looked at me and didn't say anything even the girl with her head in the toilet stopped what she was doing. There were two on the bed. One on the floor and one by the toilet. Cool I could take them all. I sized them up and with my back against the bars in the hallway, I said, who the fuck touched my Fred Barns? The one on the floor got up and started to say something "out the side of her neck". I grabbed that bitch and beat her ass. As I was beating her ass I decided to talk to her with ever punch I would say don't touch my shit and don't fuck with me do you understand. Do you understand? But she couldn't answer because my fist was in her mouth. I knew I should have stopped but I tried to put her head through the bars. Do you understand bitch? I will kill you. I kept my eyes on her friends or so called friends and smiled. Then the CO came to the other side of the bars. See there where bars then a hallway where the CO's would walk then a little window but you couldn't see outside it. It just let's light in. The CO stood in that part of the hallway and yelled stop 67 don't let me come in there. I was cool. I was tired of fighting something that didn't' fight back.

She said, go to your cell. I did. Then CO's came and then ran pass me and got the girl and left. In about an hour my cell door closed. A CO came up to my cell and said, you are going to make it hard now you stay in your cell. I thought cool. I didn't want to go anywhere anyway. I said, hey CO how's that girl.

She said, 67 do you really want to know?

I just looked at her and smiled. All you could hear is her friends talking loud. They were saying she came down here! We didn't do anything to her. She just started fighting.

66 came to my cell and sat on the floor and said damn 67. You're a bad mother fucker. I didn't respond.

She said, they would open your cell tomorrow.

I said, so I don't care if they never open it up.

I know what you mean.

The next morning my cell opened up and some of the girls that were with the girl I beat asked me if I wanted to go eat in the cafeteria and I said no. So I got some milk from the cart and went back to my cell. Then they were acting like they wanted to be my friend or something. But , I didn't want anything to do with those bitches. I found out through the jail grapevine that she was in the infirmary. Her face was really fucked up. I didn't care about that I just cared about one thing when was I getting out of this zoo. And I thought about Kendu and how I would have loved to see him again. I looked at the time and knew he would be in school. Then I thought about him at Brooklyn Tech with all those boys, and how I was in a prison with all these girls. Yeah, prison an all girl school of hard knocks. But it wasn't really that bad once I kicked someone's ass the rest was easy. I said, yeah I'm gonna call him today. I go to court Thursday and I would like him to be there. I don't know why I thought of him, shit being locked down makes your brain go to mush. About seven o'clock that night I went to the phone and called him.

On the first ring I heard him say peace. When he said peace my mouth watered.

I said, peace Kendu.

He said, Uasia.

I said, yeah.

Then he said, I miss you. I mean I think about you all the time I even told my mother how much I miss you. I've been over your house just to be close to you. I was sitting with your brother Fuel and your little sister. But, only your brother knows where you are. I thought what this guy, is a sucker I can't deal with this now.

I said, really I miss you too, oh shit why did I say that.

He said, I will be there Thursday ok.

I said, ok cool.

I couldn't believe that he would be there Thursday.

Uasia I really do think about you a lot.

I know but I got to go you know prison and all.

He said ok see you Thursday.

Ok see you Thursday.

Peace.

Peace.

Then I went back in my cell and put my face in my pillow and cried. Because I really did miss him. I also miss my brother Fuel, Raif & Craig and my little sister. I really miss my bed. But there is a chance I will never be with him or them again. You never know going to court. I still didn't know why the fuck I was in here, and I didn't have any money so I will get one of the "oh I can't afford a lawyer", lawyer. On Thursday they bought me my clothes that I got arrested in, and the CO said, if I can help it I hope you come back here. I sure would love to put you in the hole.

I said, what are you gay or something, back up. I got dressed and told 66 stay cool. She had the nerve to say I wish you would be here with me.

I said, I don't.

But, I know what she meant. A girl like that will not make it and you can't stay in your cell forever. Then the C O came and walked me over to the jail. Where there were about six other girls, and all of them were saying the same thing "I'm innocent". Yeah right that's what everyone says. I knew I was not innocent and I was not going to waist time saying that. Then a cop came to where I was sitting and said line up ladies. We did I was first. Then we walked down this long ass hallway and went into the court. We sat in the box and I looked over and there he was Kendu. Wow, he really came. He looked fine in black. He looked like he was a lawyer with his chocolate self. They called the names in alphabetical or-der. So I was first Rachel Brown.

I came and my lawyer said just listen. He was a skinny white guy and so was the judge. They said that I was charged with dis-orderly conduct for hitting a cop. My lawyer said the cop did not identify herself and Ms. Brown would have never felt the need to have to defend herself if she would have identified herself and not pushed Ms. Brown.

Then he said, that Ms. Brown had just bought a brand new hand bag and in her mind she thought that she was being robbed.

The judge looked at me and I was thinking please don't read my mind because this guy is good. I didn't have a record in Nassau county so the judge never seen me before.

He asked me what was I doing there. My lawyer said, she was

buying a bag she has a receipt.

The judge said, how do you plead.

The lawyer said, say guilty and so I did.

Then the judge said, you have to pay a fifty dollar fine. Do you have the money?

I said, no.

He said well, you have to go back to jail until you get the money.

Then Kendu stood up and came over to the lawyer. The lawyer then said, your honor she has the money.

He said, ok. You are released, Ms. Brown.

I said, yeah.

Don't come back to Nassau County.

I said, I won't. Kendu gave me a hug and we walked with the cop to the cashier. Where he paid the fifty dollars.

I said, how did you know that it was fifty dollars?

He said, his mother called and got the information.

I said, your mother.

He said, yeah.

Then we walked out of Nassau County. That was the end of Uasia and the beginning of........

CHAPTER 5

Dinequa Refinement Earth

Kendu said I have to go home. My mother wants to speak to us. I said, cool but first take me home so I can change and check in. We took the Long Island Rail Road. I asked him where is your car.

He said, he came straight from school and he doesn't like driving his car to Brooklyn.

I said, so we going to take this where.

He said, we can take this to my house.

I said, I wanted to go home first.

He said, I know I just want to pick up my car and then I will take you home so you can change and then we will go to my house.

I said, ok.

All the way to his car the train ride was not that long. And I was telling him about the fight I had in there.

He asked, man wow, you had a fight and you weren't in there that long?

I said yes.

He said, that's why I'm not going there.

Then I told him about cell 66.

He said, what was her name?

I said, cell 66. He looked at me. We got to his car just like he said we went straight to my house. When we got out the car my brother Junior walked over to me and said, what's happening sis.

I said, you didn't tell mom did you?

He said, na you know I wouldn't do that.

I said, cool. Then I went in and Kendu came with me. My mother didn't say a word she didn't even notice I've been gone for four days or maybe she did and was hoping I was dead. We went downstairs to my room. Kendu was quiet and I said, what's up you're not saying anything. Then I got in the shower and when I came out as I put on my panties and pants Kendu said "you're beautiful I don't want you to go to jail anymore". You have to change your life and I'm going to help you.

I said, "ok, but look I'm gonna make it do what it do".

He said, all of that in jail.

No.

Then I put on a shirt and Sheila came in and said, yo kuz what's up.

I said, man I hated it in there.

She said, what's up Kendu.

He said, peace.

I told her I'll be back I have to go over Kendu's house for a minute ok.

She said, welcome back kuz I want to speak to you and hear all about jail.

We all left and Kendu and I got in his car and bounced. When we got to his apartment his mother and father were there.

They said, so here you are.

I said, yeah here I am.. What's up.

She said, have a seat. So I sat on the couch with my back pressed hard against it as if I needed to cover my back. I mean how would you feel coming out of jail and being bailed out by god and now his parents are giving you the evil eye. Kendu sat next to me and I looked at him and he smiled.

His mother started out by saying we never knew anyone who went to jail before and we never knew any girls that went there either. What are you going to do with your life young lady.

I said, what do you mean?

She said, are you going to continue to go to jail?

I just looked at her.

Then Kendu said, no she won't. Then his mother said, "you can't keep getting her out".

I said, I didn't ask anyone to get me out. I could handle it. So if I'm here to hear you tell me about what's right and wrong I could leave now.

His father said, we are not trying to gang up on you.

I said, well whatever.

Then she said, do you go to school.

I said, yeah.

What grade are you in?

I said 12th.

She said, so is Ben. So you'll be graduating soon.

I said, something like that. When I said that they really looked at me. Then I said look thank you for getting me out and shit, but I really don't like all these questions, so if that's why I'm here then I should go. I'm out.

Kendu said, don't go, mom what's this all about and she looked at him.

His father said, your mother just don't want you to make any mistake in you life son.

I said, what? Do you think I'm a mistake who the fuck do you think you're talking to. Kendu put his hand over my mouth and said , well she is not a mistake and you better get used to her being around cause I'm gonna keep her. I looked at him and thought damn. Then I moved his hand from my mouth and said keep me. What? I'm some rich persons toy. What is up with you people.

Kendu said, I don't mean it like that.

I said, how do you mean it.

He smiled and said, I'll show you later.

I said, no show me now.

He said, later.

His mother said, ok well we're going now and we will see you later.

But Ben we will like to speak to you as soon as we come back. And for you young lady.

I said, yes.

Then they left. Kendu went out in the hallway for a good minute then he came back. He took my hand and lead me to his room.

He said, you got a lot to learn.

I said, whatever.

He said there is a time to talk and a time to be quiet. Then he kissed me.

I said, what do you want with me.

He said, I want to teach you how to make love to god.

I said, what?

Then he said, lets start by kissing again ok. I really thought I was a good kisser my tongue was all over the place and spit was too.

He said, wait I want you to follow me relax and let me teach.

I said, I know how to kiss.

He said, then why do we have so much spit on us.

I said, because that's what you do.

He said, follow the leader. So I did.

I took my time and followed every movement he did my tongue was slow and there was less spit. Then our lips met and shit.

I said, wow that was nice. He smiled and took me in his arms and kissed me again and my legs got weak I opened my eyes to look at him kissing me and he had his eyes opened too. Then we both smiled.

He said, now I'm going to make love to you.

I said, what?

He said, make love.

I said, I never heard it called that before.

I said, well turn off the lights.

He said, no I want to see you and I want you to see me. He started taking my clothes off and I liked the way he did it nice and slow and he kept his eyes on me. When my blouse was off he put my breast in his hand and said, the right size.

He said, how does this feel.

I said, really nice.

He said, just nice?

I said yeah.

Then he took my pants and I got scared.

He said, I'm not going to hurt you I just want to love you. I never felt like this before. I mean, I mean, man. The fear went away. Then he said, "what's this". I looked down and there it was.

I said, a bullet hole.

He said, what's this?

I said, where the bullet came out.

He said, what's this?

I said, I don't know.

He said, what's this?

I said, where the bullet came out.

Then he said, baby you've been hurt too many times. I looked down and for the first time my battle scares weren't a trophy and I wasn't proud of them. I reach for my pants to pull them back up. But he lifted my head up and I looked in his eyes and he said, no more scars ok.

And I said, ok.

Then he laid me down on his bed. And he laid on top of me. I didn't know what to do. Then I felt him inside of me. Then we made love I couldn't believe it. It was slow and good and I really felt everything. He was talking to me asking me do you like it like this, is this slow enough. No one ever asked me if I liked it and is it slow enough.

I said, yes I really like it. Then he arch my back with his hands and went deep in my sugar wall and said, now lets come together. I didn't know what he was talking about. But all of a sudden my legs started to shake and my toes started to cramp and I stared breathing faster and faster and so did he. I looked up at him and he was looking at me and then oh my goodness and then I closed my eyes and wrapped my legs around his back and held on. And it was over. I couldn't believe it. I shouted "I like it". What the fuck. I really like it.

Then he said, I hear that. And I thought oh shit did I say that out loud.

He laid on top of me and wiped the sweat off my head.

He said, so you are going to graduate this year.

I said, what?

He said, you are gong to graduate this year.

I said, I don't know. I mean what kind of shit is that to talk about after such great love making.

He said, when you graduate what are you going to do.

I said, I want to be a Happy Hooker.

He looked at me and said what?

I said, a hooker.

He said, no, why you want to be a hooker.

I said, to make money. I'll give you some when I make it.

He said, no Uasia you are not going to be a hooker.

He said, what else do you want to do.

I said, I really haven't thought about nothing else but being a hooker. Then he kissed me and said, what kind of world do you live in.

I said, what?

He said, with all these scares on you. You must have had a real hard life.

I said, my life is ok. Then he kissed me again.

I said, lets get dressed and leave, but Kendu wouldn't let me go.

He said, where are you trying to go.

I said, well it's over so I thought you wanted me to leave now.

He looked at me and smiled and said, no I'm not those other guys. I want you to stay here don't you want to stay.

I said, ok.

He laid on top of me and said, what do you want to do now. I looked away from his eyes and said, can we do it again.

He said, look at me and say what you want to say.

I said can we do it again?

He smiled and said, as many times as you want. So we did it again and oh man the feeling was even better. Then we kissed and I said I really have to go.

He said, ok I'll take you home. We started to get dressed and then my breathing started up again and I looked at him.

And he said, yes.

I said, if it's not any trouble can we do it again. And off with the clothes and on with the show.

I said, to him, Kendu can I ask you something?

He said, you can ask me anything you'd like.

I said, "what we're doing is that called Making Love?"

He said, all day long.

I said, wow.

He said, you never made love before. Then he looked at me.

I said, I had sex before but nothing like this.

He said, like what?

I said, well you make me feel so pretty you know.

He said, yeah. That's what I'm here for. To make you feel pretty, because you are pretty Uasia. We finally were able to get dressed and leave. We got in the car and my breathing started again and he said what?

I looked at him but I didn't want to ask him, no more, I thought maybe I should just shut up. Then he reached over and touched my breast and said are you ready.

I said, yeah. Then we made love in the car. We got dressed again and started to laugh.

He said, you like this don't you.

I said, I like you.

And he said, I like you too. We went to my house and was sitting on the stoop talking and laughing like there was no tomorrow.

And he said, I have to go to school tomorrow so I will see you Friday.

I said, ok and he kissed me softly and left. I couldn't believe it. I wanted him to come back I wanted him really bad. I felt like crying I really miss him. And I really didn't understand why. As I was sitting on the stoop thinking about him, Malik and Sandy came up.

They said, we heard you where out of jail

I said, yeah.

Sandy said, you are not mad at me and Nana are you.

I said, "no", they both looked at me funny. And I smiled.

Malik said, what's happening with you Uasia, I said nothing.

He said, you look different.

I said, yeah how different.

He said, I don't know but you look different.

I said, a good different or a bad different.

He said, with a smile on his face a good different. I thought yeah.

I said, so what are you guys doing.

He said, we were just coming over to see you.

I said, well shit I just got out of jail and you didn't even buy me a quart.

Malik said, I'll go and get you one if you want one.

I said, no I'm just fucking with you.

I said, well see you later and tell Nana everything is cool. I went inside and smiled, I also slept like a baby. I really slept well. When I woke up I went to school and the teacher said that I have to go to night school if I wanted to graduate and I said, ok. Night School was at Jamaica High. And I thought I would see Sheila there she was a cheerleader and sometimes she would have practice. You had to take the train to Jamaica and 165th , and walk up this big ass hill, but that was cool. I didn't mine I was thinking of Kendu all the way up and all the way down. I don't know how to explain myself but my whole body would react when I thought about him. I could still smell him. And I could still feel him. I mean is this normal?

Back to the Hood of Things;

When Friday night came Kendu came.

He said, he wanted to take me to dinner. I went in my room and got dressed. I finally got to wear my silk dress, and my patent leather shoes. But I didn't have my hair straightened but my braids where "tight". When I came upstairs with that dress on, everyone in my family looked at me like they were seeing a ghost. My brother Raif, who's name was "the King" now said, "you look real nice sis".

I said, thank you. Then I looked at Kendu and he said, you do look beautiful. Being with him made me feel like a queen. He looked at me in a way that no one else ever looked at me before.

And my father noticed it.

He said, you should see her when she sleeps. Then everyone laughed. But Kendu didn't even laugh he said, I hope I would. I was like damn this brother is bad. We got in his car and he said, I should take the bus so that everyone could see me with you.

I just smiled. We went to Beef Steak Charlie's and I liked it. We got to the door and had to wait to be seated. I really wasn't use to that. But I was cool. Then the waiter came over and said "two table for two".

And I looked around like is there anyone else here. But I was cool. Then we sat down and Kendu held my chair for me. Again I was cool. Kendu started to tell me about being a 5% nation of Gods and Earths. And about 120 lessons and then he started telling me about keeping my body ¾ covered, that the only time my body should not be covered is when he is making love to me. I could live with that. Kendu was really smart. He wanted to be a doctor and was going to Howard University when he finishes high school. He also started telling me about my stealing and robbing people and that a lady shouldn't be doing that.

I said, wow hold on there. I steal and rob because I'm good at it. If I don't do that what else would I do, I mean get a job?

He said, yeah get a job.

Whatever.

He said, Uasia is no longer your name. I'm going to name you Dinequa.

I said, what?

He said, Dinequa.

I said that is pretty where did you come up with that name.

He said well "Din" is for dinner that we are having. "E" is for equality which is 6 and this is the 6 day right.

I said right.

"Q" if for queen because you're my queen. "U" is for universe and "A" is for Allah.

That's me? I said, cool.

He said, Sunday we have a parliament where all gods and earths gather together. I want to bring you Dinequa ok.

I said, ok. We had steak and Kendu said so how do you like it here.

I said, I really do, this place is nice.

He said, and the napkins?

I said, the napkins are nice too.

I said, Kendu?

He said yeah.

I said, why are you with me? I mean you can have any girl you want. Why are you with me? I mean a hoodlum compared to you and what are you doing with me.

He said, the first time I saw you I knew you wanted to rob me. I mean every god that was in the club knew who you and your girls where. But there was something about you I just liked. And when I made love to you. You just fit. I don't know if I'm saying it right but you just fit. Like a glove in hand.

I said, like a glove in hand.

He said, yeah.

We finished eating our steaks and I felt like a queen. I loved my new name and I loved that Kendu gave it to me. Yeah I really loved that Kendu gave it to me. I really love Kendu.

Wow hold up wait a minute.

Did I just say that? Did I say that out loud. I looked over at him and no reaction. Wow, I'm glad he doesn't read minds. When we got to my house it was real dark. I said, would you like to come in my room.

He said, is that ok with your parents.

I said, I don't care.

He said, I don't want to get you in trouble.

I said, trouble is my middle name.

He said, no it's Refinement.

I said, oh yeah Dinequa Refinement. We went to my room and he sat on my bed. I looked at him and smiled.

He said, now what. I kissed him. Then I unbuttoned his shirt. Then I started kissing his chest. Then I looked at him and he said, oh yeah your learning.

I smiled and took off his pants. Then I sat on him and said hold on. He smiled and I think I did it right. But before I knew it he was on top of me. And the game was on. He spent the night I couldn't believe that I woke up with him in my bed. I just laid there staring at him. Watching him breath. Oh, man I'm really in love with him. Then I kiss him. When he opened his eyes he said peace Dinequa.

I said, peace Kendu. This man was so fine even when he woke up in the morning. He didn't have anything in his eyes that had to be wiped up. He didn't have anything on the side of his mouth that you would say wash your face. Even his waves in his hair were still there nice and tight. He was perfect. And he was in my bed. We made love that morning in my bed and every five minutes one of my brothers or my little sister would come down stairs for one thing or another. I think they noticed his car in front.

Kendu said, let me give them some attention. He stopped making love to me and said, the next one that comes down stairs I'm gonna talk to them. And wouldn't you know it my sister was the winner. She came down stairs and said hi.

Kendu said, peace what are you doing down here.

She said, she had to use the bathroom. But she didn't, she sat on the bed with us and started talking to Kendu. Before you know it my brother Fuel and The Shah were downstairs. Kendu put on his pants and sat up talking to them.

He said that the black man was the first man on the planet. And that we are the original ones. I just smiled and watched this great man teach my brothers and sister his way of life. They had so many questions to ask him. I mean the 5% was new to us. We knew gods, but none of them where like him. Then he went up-stairs with my brothers and sister and told me to get cleaned up and meet him upstairs. So I did. My parents seem to not matter that he was just coming up from my room. They didn't mind at all. He would sit and watch TV with my brothers then when he was tired he would come down stairs and go to sleep. He was doing that all the time. And I like sleeping with Kendu listening to his heart beat and watching him smile in his sleep. Could you believe it he smiled in his sleep. My mother said, that he has a radiant smile. I guess she liked it too.

Saturday he woke up and said, he will see me Sunday and then we would go to the Parliament.

I said, what do I wear?

He said, what you always wear and I will teach you how to dress after the Parliament is over ok. You'll be fine my queen. I'll be right by your side. I really didn't want to go. It was just a bunch of gods and earth. And no matter what he changed my name. For some reason I knew I wouldn't fit. And it was killing me that he may not want me after that. But he said, I love you Dinequa see you Sunday. Did he just say that he loved me. I couldn't believe that I was just thinking the same thing. I went upstairs and walked him to his car and said, what did you say.

He said, What?

I said just before you left what did you say.

He was quiet and smiled and said I love you Dinequa.

I said, yeah that's it.

He said, would you like for me to come back downstairs.

I said, please. When we went back down stairs and made love I couldn't believe that someone said they love me, I couldn't believe it. As we where making love he whispered I love you Dinequa and man did that do it. It was on then. He had to slow me down and say you have to get control of her, she gets too wet and I'll be sliding out.

I said, I can't help it, really I can't. He laid on top of me and said, I'll show you how to control her ok.

I said, what if I don't want to control her.

He said, then I will control her.

I said, Kendu you already have control over her. Then he stopped and looked at me.

I said, what?

He said, never admit that to anyone even if you love them.

I said, why?

Because it's your thing and you have to always remember there are guys in this world that will try to take advantage of you. You always be in control even with me ok.

I said, ok.

Ok, I would have said anything he wanted me to say, but did we have to stop for him to say that. Then we laughed and kept on. Eventually he left and I ran down to Sheila's house and said what do you wear to a "Parliament".

She said, a turban and a long skirt and long sleeve shirt.

I said, I don't have that.

She said, I got some material and you can use it for a turban. Sheila taught me how to rap a turban. I couldn't believe how pretty I looked it made my eyes look Chinese. I looked at Sheila and told her my new name. And she liked it. It was important to me that Sheila liked it. Because no matter what she was, she was my best friend.

She said, so what's up with you and Kendu.

I said, man Sheila he makes love to me and I can't help myself but I want it again and again. Not only that but he takes me out and talks to me about me. She smiled.

She said, well kuz looks like you're in love "hun".

I said, looks like it.

What do you think about this love thing Sheila?

She said, weren't you in love before, with Eric?

I said, I have never felt like this before, not with anyone. Not even Eric.

She said, when you had sex with Eric you didn't feel like this?

I said, no when I had sex with Eric, I didn't feel anything but hungry. Boy did we laugh. Then we started telling stories about sex and love. And I tell you Sheila is funnier than Carol Burnett. I love her too. And she loved me. But not in the same way I loved Kendu but it was love just the same.

When Sunday came Kendu called Sheila's house and said for me to meet him on Jamaica Ave. at the library. Sheila ran down to the house and I was trying to wrap that turban but I just couldn't. I was really happy to see her.

She said, that Kendu wants you to meet him at the Library.

I was like what?

Sheila said, that's what he said.

I took a deep breath and got dressed.

I put on my black Lee's and black Adidas and a black, and gold blouse and Sheila wrapped my black turban and I went to the Ave. the library was across the street from the bus terminal.

And when I got off the bus at the terminal there were a lot of people I mean 5%.

The girls, I mean queens, had on long skirts and turbans and the gods all had this little pin on them with a sun, moon and star on it.

I looked like a fish out of water. I didn't have a gun or my girls I was butt ass naked and I really felt uncomfortable. I followed everyone to the library. And I just stood in front of it. I was looking through the crowd for Kendu and there he was. When I saw him I was so happy but, he didn't see me. I stopped and looked at what I was wearing and really felt like going back home and just go to bed.... But instead I went over to where he was and I said, peace Kendu and gave him a kiss. His eyes got big and said, Dinequa don't kiss me outside. I couldn't believe it I couldn't kiss him outside.

I said, whatever I see you later.

He said, where are you going?

I said, I'm going home I knew I shouldn't have come. You just want me in bed, you really don't want anyone to see you with me. I am not Sandy, so I'll talk to you later.

He said, wait what are you talking about?

I said, don't kiss you in public. That's not what you said last night.

Then I heard these guys laughing.

They said, so Kendu who's your friend. Then he introduced me to his friends. It was Darshim who was dark skin like Kendu but, Darshim looked like a bad boy, you know with dark eyebrows slim shaped face and when he smiled it looked like he was up to something. He didn't have a queen with him, and then there was Shamir who was light skin and looked like he was 16. It looked like a pee-coat convention.

All the men had one but Kendu who was outstanding with his smile. He introduced me as Dinequa Refinement.

I said, yeah peace see ya.

Kendu took me by the hand and said, I love you, I know I

shouldn't have said that. Please forgive me. I want you to come with me. But if you want to go home then I'll see you later.

I stood there looking at him.

Then I looked at Darshim and Shamir and then back at Kendu. Who by this time looked like he was pouting.

I said, don't pout I'll come. Then he took me by the hand. We went on the train and took it to 42nd St., then took the A train to 125th. Every stop that the train made more 5% got on. There where 5% with babies that had on little "coofies" and the little queens had on long skirts and turbans. Every time one of them got on the train I smiled. I sat next to Kendu and all the gods that came around him was talking funny. I couldn't understand a word they were saying. And the earths they were all over the place. I was the only one with Lee's on. By the time we got there it was full of earth's with turbans and long skirts they call ¾ . I really felt unconformable but; Kendu took me by the hand I think he knew that. We were getting off the train and a god named Divine, he has a mustache and beard he asked Kendu why am I not dressed in ¾ and Kendu told him that I was new and that I will be dressed next time.

I said who's he?

Kendu said, let me do the talking ok.

I said, cool.

I didn't understand that. I wouldn't have told him shit. But I thought that Kendu knew what he was doing so I didn't say a word. The Parliament was on 128th st. at a school. Man there were a lot of people there and I couldn't believe how many gods and earths there where or how many children there where. But we filled that school. We went inside and Kendu was talking to another god. So I stood there waiting for him looking around at the earths and what they had on. I knew the next time they would see me I would have on ¾ also. They would never bother Kendu again. Then I heard someone call me Uasia. My heart stopped. I mean who knew me. Oh shit I hope it wasn't' someone that

I robbed. I looked around and there was Hy-Kim and his crew. Hy-Kim with a smile. I said what's up "Y" what are you doing here?

He said, I just got out of jail and I decided to come here.

I said, you just got of jail like today?

He said, no like Friday.

I went looking for you but you weren't home.

I said, my family didn't say you came by. But that was nothing new.

He said, where were you Friday?

I said, "none of your".

He just laughed. He also had the nerve to tell me about another girl named Uasia that was in Baisley projects and that she had a beef with me.

I said, I don't know that bitch. And anyway I don't roll like that anymore.

He said, no matter if you don't roll like that you're gonna deal with it.

I said, it's like that.

He said, it's like that.

I said, well when I finish here if I have time I'll go on 150th and deal with her. But He keeps looking behind me.

He said, yeah I see what are you doing with that guy.

I said, he's my god and what is it to you.

Then I said, look Y don't start anything ok.

He said, ok but that's fucked up you didn't tell me about him.

I said, tell you what? You didn't tell me about that girl with the baby either. That was left in your room with no money! And by the way your baby was sleeping in a box!

He said, "so you're going to go there".

I said, "Hy-Kim fuck this if you start with him I'll go over your house and fuck up the girl and the baby. So either we can handle this like friends or we can go into some gangster shit".

He said, what did you say. Man let me tell you my heart stop beating. I thought that Hy-Kim was gonna fuck me up. But I held my own.

I said, you heard me. You don't fuck with him and I don't fuck with her.

Then Kendu came over and said, peace to Hy-Kim.

But Hy-Kim didn't say anything. Then Kendu took my hand and we walked away. Man was he smooth. I started to explain, to tell Kendu what was going on. And he said you had a life before me as long as you don't fuck with him no more I have no beef. Kendu said, that a lot of gods are talking about you robbing people. And you and your crew. I wanted to tell Kendu about the beef that I have on 150th with the new Uasia, but I didn't want to lose him or get him involved in my shit. So I said, Kendu I will never fuck with anyone else other then you ok.

He smiled and said that was peace.

Then he said, oh yeah stop cursing. That's why I came over there because you were cursing and Shaiem said, "you listen to the mouth of that earth". I looked at Kendu and I wanted to go off for some reason, but, I couldn't think of a good one.

So I said, I'm sorry for cursing but sometimes that's the only way I talk.

He said, stick with me I'll teach you another way to talk. Then he said, the meeting is going to start soon so let's have a seat. We sat like in the middle of the auditorium. I was amazed at all the long skirts and turbans that were there. I mean and there were some really nice ones too.

I asked Kendu did they buy them.

He said, no they made them. He was looking around like he was looking for someone.

I said, are you looking for someone.

He said, yes. Oh there she is. An earth dressed in black and gold and was dark skin sat next to Kendu. I couldn't believe it, who was she? That bitch had the nerve to have on the same colors as me.

Kendu said, listen to the meeting and we will talk later. Then he looked at me right in my eyes. I think he could see my anger. I knew who she was, she was his girlfriend. I could tell by the way she looked at him. I look at him the same way. And I couldn't or didn't hear anything anyone said, I was thinking too much about who she was. After the meeting he introduced me to her, her name was Queen Niami Earth and she was Kendu's other earth.

I said, what do you mean other earth.

She said, peace in a very soft voice.

And I said, whatever.

Kendu what do you mean other earth.

He said, that god could have more then one earth.

Wow don't you think he should have told me this before.

And I thought what the fuck I should have more then one god but I didn't say that out loud. I just looked at him then I looked at her up and down and said yeah right.

Kendu, said Dinequa why don't you go with Niami after the meeting, another meeting what the fuck. After the meeting I was still angry how dare he have two girlfriends "who the fuck does he think he is". Man was I piss.

She said, Dinequa in a really soft voice let me introduce you to some of the sisters. I looked at Kendu who just looked at me with that fucking smile on his face.

I said, I don't want to meet no other sister, I really didn't want to meet you bitch.

She said, what?

I said, I really didn't want to meet you bitch. And I went to the front steps of the building and sat there waiting for this bad dream to end. Raheem one of Kendu's friend came over to me and said, peace Dinequa. I was like yeah peace to you too. He sat next to me and said you're not having fun are you?

I said, I didn't think you guys came here to have fun.

He said, you're right.

I said, look Raheem "what are you over here for?"

He said, because I saw you sitting by yourself. I was wondering what kind of women wants to be by herself. I looked at him like did he just drop some kind of jewel on me. Then I smiled and said, you're very cleaver.

He said, I know. Then we laughed. Kendu came over to where we were sitting, with that Niami bitch.

He said, let me take you home

I said, yeah. Then the three of us started walking to the train. And the three of us got on the train. And the three of us sat down. And before the three of us got too fucking comfortable.

I said, so what's up?

I said, let me tell you something right now Kendu if she comes over my house I will fuck her up.

Kendu said, I thought I told you to stop cursing.

I said, that was before or after you and Niami.

He said, Dinequa I am not going to talk about this on the train!

I said, so I don't care if you never talk about it. I wanted her to say something so bad anything so I could have a reason to fuck her up. But the sister was cool she didn't even look my way. When we got to 42nd St. I stood up to get off then I looked behind me and Kendu said, for me to go home and he was going to take her home and come see me later.

I said, no you won't. Don't come see me later fuck you and this 5% shit. And I got off the train and waited for another train. I really thought he was going to get off the train and come after me. But he didn't. He just sat with her. Then he was talking to her properly trying to explain my savage ways. I was, I was, I don't know how I was but, I missed him already.

When I got on the next train gods and earths were on there too. I just found a seat by myself and thought about Kendu and how I will never see him again. When I got off the train I walked home from the ave. Thinking and walking. By the time I made it home I have walked myself up to angry. I was "vext". I went downstairs and sat on the bed.

Sheila came over to ask me about the meeting. I told her about Niami and Sheila even thought it was bull shit. I was thinking about the last time he was in my bed and how sleeping would not be the same without him. I was really upset. Then I remember that I had some weed so I rolled a joint and got high. Then everything was better. Sheila and I were thinking "wow I should go get some munchies". I mean really what is a good high without munchies. So we went to the corner store on Keeseville and when we walked in Kendu was coming out.

I said, what are you doing here?

He said what are you doing here? I thought I told you to go home and I will be there. I looked around thinking that she was there.

I said, where's your earth.

He smiled and said, I thought she was in front of me. Sheila said, well I'm going in the store.

I said I'll be right there.

Kendu said, is there something you want to say to me.

I looked at him and said, I don't want you to have two earths and I don't like it.

He said, really.

I said, really and if you are going to be with her then you can't be with me.

He said, really.

I said, really.

He said, I guess I'll go home then.

I said, I guess you will. I felt like all this and now nothing. The finest man in the world Mr. Perfect, and all I will end up with is nothing after a year. Then he said, if I didn't tell you what then.

This mother fucker thinks I want him so bad. Fuck him.

Then he said, If I tell her that I couldn't be with her anymore, and that I wanted to be with you and that you where more important to me. But if you want me to leave then I guess I will.

I said, you told her that.

He said, If. I love you Dinequa.

I said, I love you too and that's cool with me.

Then he said, well we are going to have to get you dressed in ¾ and you have to get your diploma from school and then get a job is that ok with you.

I said that's ok with me.

Wait a minute did he just con me. He never said, that he didn't have her anymore. Did he tell her to get lost? Oh, well what the fuck he's here now.

The next day I went to school and made a quick dash for the principals office. I couldn't believe it but I went right up to her and said I need a diploma.

The principal said, that I have to get these papers signed by night school first. I told her I'll be right back. I went up to the night school and said, I need someone to sign these papers so that I can get my diploma and they signed it. It was just that simple no extra classes no extra nothing. No beef. Just signed, sealed and delivered. I went back to Andrew Jackson and showed it to the principal and she gave me a diploma.

I said, so I can leave the school right.

She said, well Rachel you can go. I was like cool. I went home and chilled.

My father said, what are you doing home.

I said, I went and got my diploma.

He said, you what?

I said, my diploma then I opened this blue pretty folder that they gave me and showed my father my diploma. He looked at it then looked at me.

Then he said, did you steal it.

I said, no see the principal signed it and everything.

He said, well "I be damn".

I said, I gathered that.

Later that day Kendu came over and I said, here's my diploma now what.

He said, how did you get that?

I said, I went to school and they gave it to me. He looked so surprised.

I said, what?

He said, how did you do that?

I said, well I knew they didn't want me back at that school for another year.

Hold up wait a minute. I know you're reading this saying that's not funny they just gave her a diploma. Well they did. And at the time I did think it was funny.

Then we laughed.

He said, ok now you have to get a job.

I said, a job?

He said, yeah how do you think you could buy material for your $3/4$.

I said, I could steal it. I've been stealing.

He said, no Dinequa I don't want you to steal anymore ok.

I said, ok what's the big deal in stealing everyone does it.

He said, not me. Ok.

I said, ok don't bite my fucking head off.

He said, that's another thing stop cursing.

I said, look now let me curse I won't steal so let me curse.

He said, that's not lady like please try not to.

I said, I'll try. I did say that with my fingers cross behind my back. Having a diploma made my whole family want to see it. Even Sheila came over to see it.

She said, it's real

I said, I know.

She said, you do a lot of things kuz but this tops them all.

I said, ain't it cool. So the next day I woke up and looked for a job. We had this program called Man Power that will help you get a job. The lady there said, you have no skills. You can't type or answer phones you can't even file so what can you do.

I said, well I can learn.

So she looked at me then said, well I do have a job opening that will train you it's called Carefreeze Plastics Company. They are located off Jamaica Ave.

Do you know where that is?

I said, yeah.

So she gave me a blue slip and sent me there.

She said, she will call them to let them know I was coming.

When I got there a woman (Spanish) sat me down and started asking me have I ever been here before.

I said, no.

Have you or anyone in your family ever worked for Carefreeze Plastics Co. before.

I said, no.

Well this is piece work. The more straws you make the more you get paid. It is 10 cent a straw and if you last for thirty days it will go up to 25 cents. Let me show you how to work the boards and straw.

Man this place really smells and it was really dirty. There were boxes and straws everywhere. Then she showed me this hot board with nails in it. She took some plastic and started to weave it around and said, before you remove the straw wait or the straw will melt and you have to start over. Let me see you do it.

I said, ok. I tried about three times and then I got it.

She said, you're good you'll go far here. The boss will be here tomorrow and you can come in about 8:00am don't be late.

I said, see you tomorrow. I was on the Ave and there was nothing for me to do so I went in the material store and stole some new material. I mean I had to celebrate. I just got my diploma and a job. I went home and told everyone that I have a job at Carefreeze Plastics Co. everyone was "syked". But no one was more excited then my Kendu. Who celebrated by taking me shopping for material.

I said, you want to take me where?

He said, shopping for material..

I couldn't tell him that I just stole some black material from the store.

So I said, ok.

Where are we going?

He said, I saw this fabric store on the Ave. Have you been there? Then he looked me in my eyes like he knew the answer.

I said, yeah I've been there.

He said, have you stolen anything from there? I looked him in his eyes and said no. "I thought about you".

Then he said, good so let's go there.

Lying to him was for his own good. I didn't want to hurt his feelings. I mean he really wanted to buy me something and if he knew I stole from there it may make a good day bad. At least that's what I told myself. I picked out this green and white checked material, and some elastic. Then we went for pizza. Because we didn't eat pork. I mean you had to read everything to make sure it didn't have pork in it. And even soap had pork in it. So we washed in peppermint soap. And even toothpaste had pork in it. So we brushed or teeth with Tom's tooth paste. I mean we lived in the health food store. By time we got home we were full and I was hyped. We went down stairs and Kendu asked me can you sew?

I said, I never did it before but I'll try.

He said well go to sleep early to get to work and I will be there to pick you up.

What time do you get off.

I said 4:00.

He said, cool.

Then 4:00 it is. I didn't want him to leave but he had to go to school. When Kendu had to go to school he didn't fuck around. He went to school.

I said, I will have on my ¾ when you pick me up.

He said, well I know it takes time to sew so whenever you finish I'll see it.

I said, I will finish today and I will wear it tomorrow.

He smiled and said, see you Dinequa, kissed me and left. Well as soon as he left I started to cut out the material. It felt like second nature. I cut and sew by hand and make a ¾ skirt and matching vest no pattern, no help, just did it. I didn't have enough for a turban but I took what I had left and added some white and "wala" it was done, a hand made turban. I finished in less then two hours. The first thing I really made. I picked out a white shirt and black shoes, Fred Barns those where the only shoes I had. I wish I had white or green shoes yeah green shoes with a matching bag. I had to make note of this: steal green shoes and matching bag. Well black would have to do.

The next morning I took a shower and got dressed. I felt like a princess. No like a queen. I was "fab". When I got upstairs I had a smile on my face that the world could see. My father said, you look nice, where did you get that from?

I said, I made it.

He said, you did?

I said, yeah.

He said, where are you going and my mother said she going no where. No where it was just like her to shoot me down when I was feeling good. I just didn't know why it still hurt.

I said, I'm going to work. I got a job at Carefreeze Plastics Co.

She said, how did you do that, you don't have a diploma.

I said, yes I do. I went down stairs and got my diploma and came back up and threw it at her and said, huh. I had never been more proud of me than, I was then. I remember when my mother use to say you'll never be nothing but a hoe. Only the good dye young and that bitch is not going no where and my favorite she'll be in jail for the rest of her life.

She always said that when I got arrested but I was always home. I think I was always home just to piss her off.

She said, well no matter what you do you will never be nothing at the end.

I took my diploma back down stairs and when I came back upstairs my father said, I'm very proud of you.

I looked at him and said, thanks dad. I don't know why but I think my father was finally getting tired of her shit.

Anyway.

I went to my first day of work and was so proud. I walked in, and from the outside it didn't look like a factory. But on the inside it had a smell of burnt plastic. And a lot of women where there. I was the only one with ¾ on, but I was the best looking one if I had to say so myself.

The boss was a little dark haired white guy with bushy eyebrows. I mean they where bushy they almost touched each other.

He said, ok so you have to work over here. It was near his office.

He said, if I do not make five boxes I will not be there tomorrow. So I looked at my working space and said, lets do it. It took me about five tries and then I was off. I not only made five boxes I made seven. At the end of the day I was tired and I smelled like burnt plastic. The boss would meet us at the door and tell you how many boxes you've done and you where suppose to write it down, to keep track of how much money you've made. But I already had that on track and I have already spent the money before I got paid.

He said, you will get paid on Friday see you tomorrow.

I smiled and said, peace.

Kendu was outside waiting for me. I was so hype. I told him how the boss looked and that I get paid on Friday. He was so proud. By the end of the week I had made almost 12 boxes. I got paid $350.00 for the week. I ran to the car and said look Kendu $350.00 in bills. We didn't get paid by check and I was glad.

He said, well let's go across the street and open you up a bank account.

I said, ok. I had no idea what or why I took fifty of my dollars and gave it to some women so that she could give me a booklet. I took that booklet and looked at Kendu he said, what.

I said, what, nothing why did I do that.

He said, you never had a bank account before. I just looked at him sometimes when Kendu would ask me a question like you never or you haven't it really made me feel funny. It sometimes made me feel like I wasn't', I don't know, it just made me feel funny.

He said, well what we are going to do is take fifty dollars every time you get paid and then you would have a lot of money. And when you get older you can buy a car or a house or whatever you want.

I said, so what now.

He said. Lets go shopping. Kendu always had money too. He use to come downstairs & bag up ounces. But, he wasn't a big weed dealer, just enough to buy those Ballys. And boy did we go shopping. I had bought four pairs of shoes, material that will last for ever. And by the way Kendu didn't believe I made this outfit by hand. When we got home I had a lot of boxes and you know it felt good not to steal it. It really felt good to walk up to the cashier and pay for it. I had the time of my life. We went straight down stairs and I even had money left over. He made it his business to watch me sew. So I did, I made two skirts right in front of him.

He said, you know you're good at this, I wonder what you can do with a sewing machine. I just smiled and kept sewing. He always knew what to say.

He said, lets go out today to celebrate your first pay day.

I said, well I'm kind of tired.

He said, that's ok how about tomorrow.

I said, yeah that would be good. When Saturday came I was so excited. My brother Fuel said, wow sis you really look good.

I said, peace.

He smiled and I knew that day my brother was proud of me. I really looked like an earth. We went to the movies that Saturday and watched "The Mac" with "Richard Pryor". It was a good movie and I loved it.

Kendu said, that the Mac was good, but he liked the brother in it, because the brother was trying to keep them out of trouble and clean up the neighborhood. I liked the Mac he was fine.

He said, you would like the Mac, hey you asked.

Then we would go to our favorite steak place. Beef Steak Charlie's and I ordered what I always order steak medium rare with shrimp and broccoli, and Kendu got steak well done with potatoes. I really loved Beef Steak Charlie's it was right on Broadway and everyone was there, Plus when you left you could go around the corner and buy a bag of weed from the Harlem Boys or walk a little ways down and get your picture taken. The gods had the picture thing sewed up, especially Sincere. He was a tall dark goofy looking brother and Kendu really liked him. Sincere was full of jokes like "The Jerk". We even got two pictures for five dollars.

Kendu said, next Saturday we will go see "Dawn of the Dead" and I want you to look real pretty ok earth.

I said, ok god. But I didn't know why he said that. I thought that I really looked pretty today. And like always after a movie or after anything that we did we went over to my house and to my bed and of course I strived for that feeling again. And like always the feeling came and came and came. Monday went fast and so did the week when I got paid. I went over and put fifty dollars in the bank now I had $100.00. Kendu was right wow that banking thing was really working out. Kendu picked me up with Raheem they where telling me about Saturday and that other earths where coming with their gods too. It was going to be a big thing. So I told Kendu that I had to get some material and I wanted to buy some shoes and I need to go to 42nd street.

He said, ok let's drop off Raheem at the library. I couldn't wait anymore.

I said, Everlasting Lord Kendu God Allah are you ready.

He said, yeah. We went to my favorite material store.

I said, Kendu what are you wearing.

He said, black and white.

He said, he had this black and white suit and some new "croc" shoes. So I brought black and white pinstriped material that had white silk in it. Then I went and brought some black croc from the store on the corner of 42nd at this real nice shoe store. Then we went to Stetson hat store next to the train station. And I bought Kendu a velour hat. All the gods where wearing them.

He said, wow thanks earth. Then we went home he dropped me off first and then he went home. I wanted to start sewing. I really got good at this sewing stuff to the point that everyone use to look at it and swear I bought it. The next day was Saturday I worked on my 3/4. I worked all day I didn't even go outside once. The ¾ was easy. I just did a skirt with a vest but the blouse was hard. I had to take it off and fit it better so I decided to do it with short sleeves and a v neck. I just put cuffs on the sleeves, yeah, cuffs on a short sleeve shirt, cool. When I tried it on it was perfect. Then I took a shower and put on my black silk underwear. I just got out of the dry Cleaners and my Tabu. Then I got dress boy did I look nice if I had to say so my self.

Kendu came over and I knew he was there because my little sister was so excited she really thought that he looked nice. Then I came upstairs as I walked upstairs the ¾ just flowed, it was like I had on a wedding gown. I felt so, so, I don't know how I felt the feeling was so wonderful that I was afraid of it. Like I was going to wake up and it will all be gone. Kendu was in the living room watching TV and talking to my sister. When he saw me he stood up and just stared at me.

I said, peace

Peace, you look great earth.

I said, so do you god.

My mother even said you guys look like you are getting married are you.

I said, no mom we are going to the movies.

Kendu walked up to me and smiled and kissed me on my cheek and said are you ready.

I said, yes. When we walked out side my brother Fuel and his friend Felix were standing there.

My brother said, sis you look great.

I said, peace.

Then he opened the car door for me and I sat down. When he got in the car he looked at me and said Dinequa you are so beautiful. I'm so proud of being with you today. Then he laughed and said, we are going to be the best looking couple there.

I smiled and said we are already the best looking couple.

He smiled and kissed me and said, let's go.

I said, yeah let's go get them.

Kendu took his car, and parked it at the bus terminal parking lot. Then we went across the street where the other gods and earths were. I felt like a queen and Kendu was my king. Everyone said, how nice we looked and the earths couldn't believe that I made it by hand so they checked the hem and back of my blouse and said, she did make this by hand. Everyone was there, it looked like a convention. Oh wow, earth this is nice you really could sew. I was just smiling from ear to ear. Kendu took me by the hand and we walked to the train station. It was like thirty of us. And we all looked nice. When we got to the train none of us paid to get on the train.

Kendu said, Dinequa and I were just like a glove and hand and then we went through. When we got on 42nd street there were lights all over the place.

42nd street was buzzing with people but we were the gods and earths. And we walked like gods and earths. The 85%, those that the gods state were not righteous, just stopped and stared. The gods where well pressed and the earths where polished. We looked great and we knew it. Even the police moved out of our way. And I couldn't believe it but I was with this. We went to the movies and it was crowded. All the seats where taken so we had to sit on the steps. Boy when the movie got going it was so scary that I put my head in Kendu's chest. It was so scary that someone in the movies screamed monster is coming. Boy we almost jumped out of our skin. Then like thunder we all started to laugh. After the movies we went to Beef Steak Charlie's. With almost thirty people Beef Steak Charlie's sat us together in a big room they had in the back. Man I looked around and everyone was happy and laughing. The food was "tight". They even gave us extra salad and bread sticks. Then it was off to take pictures. I loved my picture and Sincere said, wow you two look like you just got married.

Kendu said, yeah everyone says that. Boy we were the talk of the town with our outfits. Then we all met at the train station and everyone went home.

Kendu took me to his house. I haven't been to Kendu's house in a long time. I was beginning to think I couldn't come over anymore and that he didn't want to tell me. But that was peace. As he parked the car, I said, wow I haven't been here in a while.

He said, yeah I know.

Then he opened my door and took me by the hand and we went to his place. And his brother was there he said, oh wow you guys look so nice. Where did you come from?

Kendu told him everything and I showed him the picture and he said let me have it. I'm going to blow it up and I'll give it back.

We said, ok.

Then we went to Kendu's room and made love but this time Kendu put on music the "Whispers" and we made love to music. When the song Lady came on Kendu made love to me while singing.

As he was singing in my ear, and I was feeling his breath on my neck, my heart started beating so fast. I couldn't believe this gorgeous man was with me. This felt so good, it's not like it's my first time, but it's my best time....

Then all of a sudden he started talking about the earth, knowledge and the moon, he was telling me all kinds of things, how we could build. And like "I love you, I hope you love me..." This guy is really killing my mood. I don't know what he was talking about, why doesn't he just SHUT THE FUCK UP! And just go back to singing and sex.

He must have felt the difference in me, because he got back to singing the song and got back into the groove.

By time he got to Lady, I melted in his arms. Oh what a night. When he took me home I couldn't believe how nice my day and night went. I could have died and went to heaven. Monday was another day at work only this time I went to the bathroom and the boss was feeling up this girl. I mean rubbing her breast and everything. The look on the girls face was of fear and the boss looked like the devil. When they saw me he stopped. When I came out the bathroom the girl was there. She was a little Spanish girl who looked like someone's mother.

I said, are you ok.

She said, yes. He does that to everyone.

I said, what he never did that to me.

She said, well if he does just let him so you can keep your job. He fired the last girl who said something about it. I didn't really understand some of what she said, she had a heavy accent. I couldn't believe that someone would let that happen to them, so they could keep their job. It's just a Carefreeze Plastics Co. job. She just looked at me. I went back to my station and the boss came over to me. And said that the job would be moving at the end of the month to Long Island and do I want to come.

I said, I have to ask my husband about that, but I will let you know.

When Kendu came to pick me up I told what had happened.

And he said, he never did that to you did he?

I said, hell, I mean no.

He said, well this is a good job and Long Island is not far so you can go.

I said, ok I'll tell him tomorrow but I didn't see him the next day the only time I saw him was Friday, when he gave us our checks.

On Friday I said, my husband said it's ok for me to go to Long Island and he gave me a look like a wolf waiting for the prey. But I didn't think nothing of it. I just went to the bank and waited for

Kendu. When he came we went shopping.

He said oh yeah my mother wants to see us tomorrow, so I'll come over and pick you up.

I said, ok. All that night I wondered what his mother wanted. I haven't seen her in a long time. And I know that she didn't like me. When he picked me up I had on another "Dinequa original", I knew that when I meet his mother she would look me up and down.

And when she got to the down my patent leather shoes would blind her. I put Vaseline on them.

She said oh Dinequa you look so nice. I like the way you are dressing now.

I said, thank you. I knew that it must have hurt her to admit that but I took it like she gave it.

Then she said, have a seat. I know my son loves you so I have a present for you.

Then she gave us two tickets we both were like what is this?

She said, these are ticket to the A Ballet and I want you two to go there. We were like when?

She said, tonight at eight.

We looked at each other and said ok. I mean the only play I ever went to was "Fidler On The Roof" with my class. I loved it, but had to act like I didn't, to remain cool. So I was really game for this I was hoping that it was like the one I've already seen. It was off Broadway and it looked like a big ass movie theater with velvet everywhere. Kendu showed the door man our tickets and he showed us to our seats. We were not use to it. He really showed us to our seats. Sitting around everyone was dressed up and quiet. As soon as a guy came out in tights we knew that we were not going to like it. By the end of the first half, Kendu and I had been told three times to be quiet. We couldn't stop laughing at the boys with tights. Here we were kids from the streets how were we suppose to act. We were use to 42nd St. movies where everyone talks and laughs out loud. No this place everyone had to be quiet and clap at the same time.

When the lights came on we couldn't wait to leave. But they said, this is just the first half, and there was another half more to the play we were like ah bye. Then we went to the store and bought o'e.

He said, ok we have to go to my house and tell my mother about the play.

I said, what we didn't like it do you want me to tell her that.

He said, yeah why not.

That was one thing about Kendu that was different from me. I'll lie in a minute. But not Kendu he will tell you the truth whether you want to hear it or not. Then we went to his house his mother said, what are you doing back so soon.

We said, we didn't like it.

She said, why?

Then Kendu said, because they all had on pink panties. Then I laughed. She looked at us like we didn't have any class. But we didn't care.

She said, so what do you guys like.

Kendu said, with a smile on his face the Whispers and I laughed. When anyone would ask us what we like we would say the Whispers meaning sex.

His mother said, that she likes their music too. And I really laughed. Kendu nudged me and said, Dinequa. I was like sorry. Then his mother went to the room and Kendu drove me home. But not before we did the "nasty" in the car. We couldn't help it, we did the nasty everywhere. I mean don't even leave us alone for a minute because we would do the nasty. And the nasty we did well, we fit like a glove. That's one thing about us we were good with each other. We where good not only making love, but with each other. Like we were the same person.

Monday I went to work and everything was ok, but on Thursday the boss asked me about going to Long Island, I said it's ok I could go, I thought I told you this before.

He said, yes you did.

On Friday he came over to me I was working on my straws

and he touched me on my breast. I grabbed his hand and turned him around and said, don't you every put your hands on me. Then I don't know why, but he tried to move his hand or tried to grab mine and I put his hand on the hot burner and said, don't put your hands on me you get it cracker.

Then he said, get out of here.

I said not without my pay.

He said, you burned me, you black bitch and I snapped.

I smacked him right in the face then the girl that hired me said please here's you check.

I said, you should not have this cracker touch you. I know that he touches you girls here. Do you need the money so bad that you would let him touch you.

She said, yes.

He said, call the cops. I just knew I would be in jail. But the girl said no let her just leave. So I left and smiled. Then he had the nerve to say "you're fired".

I said, yeah right white boy. I went over to the bank and put my fifty dollars in it. Then waited for Kendu at Burger King. He came up with Raheem and I told him what had happened, he laughed and said, well we have to get you another job.

Raheem said, why don't she go to the trade school on Merrick Blvd.

I said, yeah, I'll do that on Monday. I started business school at "O I C" they taught me how to type and file. And they would give you money for going there. I thought that it would be cool. They also said that they could get you a job or an interview after you graduated. I thought ok. On March 3 it was Kendu's birthday. And I wanted to get him something special so I went to the bank and took out fifty dollars then I went to 42nd st. to Stetson Hat Store and bought him a black derby in size seven.

The man said, I had great taste and that Kendu would be very happy with it. I thought yeah. They put the derby in a hat box that was just as nice as the hat.

When Kendu came over I gave him the hat and took him to dinner not to Beef Steaks Charlie's but to the new place. Tabs. They did your steaks on a flame grill and they let you see them do it. Kendu was very impressed. When we made love that night Kendu was saying that he wanted me to have his seeds.

I said ok. Boy did we try. We tried with pillows under my back and boy did that hurt. Then we tried with my legs in the air. Then we tried by Kendu staying inside of me for about twenty minutes, and trust me it was the whole twenty minutes. Then on March 13th Kendu came and picked me up and took me to Sylvia's in Harlem. Man Harlem was cool. Sylvia's had a lot of chicken but also a lot of pork, so all we could eat was chicken. But she had nice cakes and then they came over to our table and sang happy birthday to me. I was so happy; I smiled until I got a headache. I didn't know but me and Kendu had a lot in common. The two years that we were together I didn't remember that we both are Pisces and we both loved each other. I loved him so much.

I graduated from O I C in June and they set me up on a job interview with New York Telephone Company. The guy that interviewed me was in a wheel chair and I played into it. But really all I did was be myself (my new self). I helped him with his wheel chair. I helped him answer the phone. Then I sat down and talked to him.

I asked him how he got in the wheel chair.

He said, that he was born like that. I didn't know that people was born that couldn't walk.

He said, that he really appreciates me asking him about the wheel chair.

He said, that most people just stared.

He said, that he likes me and that the Phone company needs more people like me to work there.

I said, so I got the job.

He said, yes. I screamed and said thank you.

He said, no Rachel thank you.

When I told Kendu that I'll be working at the phone company in the World Trade Center he was like wow Dinequa how do you get such good jobs.

I said, you baby, it's you.

He kissed me and I loved it by time August came we decided not to speak about having a baby again. And just hope that it happens.

That summer Kendu and his family went to a lot of places like Hawaii. I didn't even know that black people went to Hawaii. He bought me a tee shirt from Maui. I was like ok, but I will only wear this around you.

He said, I hope so. Then one day Kendu came to me and said, that he would be going to college and it's in Washington. Howard University.

My heart stopped and I couldn't breath. Ever since we met we've been together (other then me going to jail). I was like I didn't even know you graduated.

He said, yeah, I didn't think you wanted to go.

I said, you are leaving me.

He said, no Dinequa I'll be here and I will see you every weekend.

You will be working so by time you finish working I will be here. I couldn't say nothing. I just knew that it was over, my world would be over. But Kendu didn't want me to believe it. I cried that night. He made love to me every day and he picked me up everyday. I think he was trying to make me feel better. But it didn't work. How do you feel better when the man that made you a women, the man that made love to you like no one every did. The man that was always with you, the only man that you love is leaving. By the last day, the last day he left I couldn't come with him. I couldn't understand why, I couldn't go with him.

His mother and father where taking him there. I just couldn't believe it. Two years we where together, now no more. His parents don't know how much we loved each other. Can't they see. I wouldn't have finished high school if it wasn't for him, and now two years later. He finished high school and leaves. This sucks. That day I left work and came home on the train and bus something that I haven't done in a long time I felt so alone.

I sat on the stoop and my mother came out and asked me what was wrong. I told her about Kendu leaving.

She smiled and said, I told you that you will never be happy, that you will die alone. At the end you will be nothing and have nothing. I just looked at her and decided to go to bed and study my 120 lessons. And looked at the pictures of Kendu and I. I must have fallen asleep because someone was kissing me. I opened my eyes and it was Kendu. I grabbed him and hugged him.

I said, you're not going.

He said, yeah but my parents drove me here to say peace.

He said, Dinequa tell me not to go and I won't. But I knew not to say that, I knew he had to go.

He wanted to be a doctor and we needed black men to be doctors to take care of us.

So I said, no Kendu you have to go. You are god and you are the cream, you have to rise to the top.

He said, walk me upstairs and there they where, Kendu's mother and father and my mother and father. I wish I was a fly on that wall.

Kendu said, bye to my mother and father and I walked him to the car, kissed him and then he was gone. My Kendu was gone.

That week went on and on, like Friday would never come. I did what Kendu taught me I put fifty dollars in the bank and went shopping with the rest. I started buying things for my brothers and sister. Now since I didn't have Kendu no more. Kendu was a man of his word, he was here on the weekends and my hope was back my love was back, my god was back. He told me how he missed me and that I should come up and see him sometimes and I did. If he was not coming to New York I was going to Washington. He stayed off campus with this boy, and we would stay in bed and make love all day. He even had a blow up picture of him and me over his bed. I loved making love to him, especially with my picture on the wall above us. I would come home in all kinds of cars. One day I decided to take the gold Bonneville for a ride while Kendu was in my bed sleeping. I snuck out and got in the car then I looked over to the window and there was my little sister.

I said, what are you doing here?

She said, I want to go.

I said, no now go in the house.

She said, I'll tell and I knew she would, she was good at telling. So I opened the door and let her in. We went to the store on Linden and Farmers and got in an accident and I just pulled off and kept going. Boy did we laugh.

I said, yo sis don't tell ok.

She looked at me like yeah I won't . But I didn't care if she did. I used to steal cars all the time and take her with me. She really enjoyed riding with me. And I really enjoyed being with her. My little sister. Then we went in the house and Kendu never mentioned it. I did think he knew I stole the car and I know he knew that I got in an accident but he didn't say a word. And that's what I loved most about him he never said, anything bad about what I did and never got mad at me either. I mean, he used to tell me that I was wrong, but he never just got mad. Kendu used to come see me every weekend and that was cool but I really wanted to go to Washington. I mean, I would love to surprise him. I've never been to a big college before or to any college before. And I thought that it would be nice to come and see him. You know to meet his friends. So I worked the whole week without stopping or taking lunch so that my paycheck could be full. Then I bought some material and made me a red and a dark blue ¾ and I bought Kendu a white derby. I packed my bags and got on a bus to Washington to Howard University. I was so excited I knew where he was. I knew the room he would be in, and I just asked some students where the hotel was. Which the cab had no problem finding. I stood there in front of this hotel that the students would stay in. It was called off campus. And it was hype. It had a big lobby with a couple of couches in it. I've never been in any place like this before. And I couldn't wait for Kendu to see me. I got in the elevator and pressed his floor. Then I got off and made a left and went to his room. But he wasn't there. So I waited in the lobby. I was hoping that he wasn't at my house. Oh shit if he was at my house and I was here oh my goodness. I sat there about twenty to thirty minutes watching people come and go. And was hoping that I didn't miss him. I just sat there holding his hat in my hand hoping to see my man. I spotted him with some guy and I walked over and said, peace.

He looked surprised to see me but then he smiled and said, peace. But he didn't introduce me to the guy and I didn't mine. I just figure that he was an 85% and Kendu didn't want me to meet him. He took my luggage and asked me what was I doing there.

I said, I just wanted to surprise you. You come over to see me all the time so. I just wanted to see you for once. Then I gave him the hat box.

He said, let's go to my room and I'll look at it there. Then we went upstairs to his room.

He said, Dinequa I have to take a shower and I'll be out.

I said, would you like for me to join you.

He said, no I'll be out.

I said, ok.

Which was strange, because by now we would be having sex on the floor. But I didn't take it so serious I just thought he was tired. While he was in the shower the door bell rang. So I went and answered it. There was a dark skin girl with her hair in curlers with a pink bathrobe on standing there.

I said, yeah.

She said, you're Dinequa!

But she said it like she couldn't believe that I was there, like I was a ghost or something.

I said, yeah how did you know that. She pointed to my picture.

I said, what do you want.

She said, nothing, I'll come back later.

I said peace.

She said, bye. I stood at the door for a minute and thought it in my brain. What just happened. What's going on? Then I felt this funny feeling in my stomach like I was going to get sick. I just swallowed and held my breath and sat down. When Kendu came out of the shower I took a deep breath and said, a girl came by but she didn't say who she was.

Then Kendu sat next to me and said Dinequa remember when you had that abortion.

I said, yeah.

Well when you told me about what happened to you , I knew that I wanted you to have my baby, but we've been making love for years now and you're not pregnant. I think they done something to you.

I felt a tear come to my eye.

I said, Kendu what are you saying are you saying that I'm a moon, a dead planet.

He said, no. Dinequa you are not a dead planet. You are and always will be my earth. But, Dinequa remember that girl that was at the door.

I said, yeah.

He said, she is having my baby.

I felt the earth move.

He said, I thought I couldn't have kids.

I felt the sky tumbling down.

He said, but that doesn't mean I don't love you. I do Dinequa I just want a seed.

I couldn't believe this. I was being punished for having an abortion that I didn't even want to have. I can't have kids.. Oh I tried to keep the tears from falling but I couldn't breath. I just got up and picked up my pocket book and luggage and walked out of the room down the hall and down the stairs. By time I got to the lobby Kendu was there.

He said, please Dinequa don't leave me.

I said, Kendu you left me remember.

He said, well let me drive you home ok. Then he went upstairs to get dressed.

But I couldn't wait for him. It felt like everyone in the lobby knew except me. The pain was too great my legs, my feet, my arms, my heart the pain was too great. I couldn't stand there anymore. So I left I got in a cab and went to Greyhound. I was waiting for the bus to come and there he was.

Dinequa please let's talk. I just held on him and said, oh Kendu what am I going to do? What do you want me to do. I don't know what to do.

He said, Dinequa just love me that's what I want you to do. Just love me ok. Then we kissed and we went to the car. And he drove me home. When we got home I just went downstairs to my room without saying anything. Kendu came downstairs and we cried together. Then we made love, but making love to him was different, it was like we were making love, like we will never see each other again. Not like we use to. We held each other so tight. And we cried while making love. Then we held each other tight again. Then I went to sleep and when I woke up he was gone.

Kendu started to stay away more and more and on the weekends I refused to go down there, so we didn't see each other that much. I started stealing again, but this time I did it in ¾ . I hung out with other earths that stole too. Then I saw Angelfire she was out of jail. I couldn't believe it. I drove her home on my new stolen moped. She loved it.

She asked me what's up with the outfit. I told her that I was an earth and that my god was away in college.

She said, ok. How's that working out for you.

I said, fucked up. He's got another girl pregnant.

She said, so you steal mopeds now.

I said, yeah.

She said, do you get paid for it.

I said, no but I love stealing them and they get you here and there.

She said, well if I'm going to steal mopeds then I'm going to get paid. Man we started stealing and it was funny they were like hey the earths are stealing mopeds. I was like everyone knew it was us. People use to come over to my house and ask for their mopeds back. And I use to go to the door and curse them out and say yeah I took it so what the fuck are you going to do about it. Get the fuck out of here and slam the door. It would shut right in their faces. Then one weekend Kendu came up and said, that the girl had an abortion because he would never love her. Because he loved me. I don't know why but it just didn't faze me. I was not impressed. I mean it was too late.

It was like Al Green said, how can you mend a broken heart. How can you stop the rain from falling down?

We made love but I controlled it and Kendu felt it.

He said you're different Dinequa.

I said, really so are you.

He said, what have you been doing.

I said, nothing working you know what I've done.

He said, "I heard you're stealing mopeds".

I said, yeah and. Damn right I was stealing mopeds. I had a crew of girls Mary, Angelfire, Nana , and Arabia, that's what Malik started calling Sandy. We wore long skirts and we were clean. Everyone wore long skirts but Angelfire. But that was cool. See we use to walk up and see a moped or asked if we could get a ride then the snatch was on. Stealing mopeds was easy. Like taking candy from a baby.

1. No one expect us to steal moped, not 5% girls.
2. You didn't need to do anything but get on and ride.
3. We were good at hit and run.

Yeah we hit and run. Just like I thought Kendu did me. Hit and run. I was with him when he was just a high school student. He use to bag weed on my bed. I stopped Hy-kim from killing him. Now he's this big college guy and what.

He said, you stole one in Harlem.

I looked at him I said, yeah I needed to get home.

He said it belong to Little Harlem Boys.

The Little Harlem Boys was a gang in Harlem, NY who worked for a famous drug dealer that the streets knew as Sledge.

One day we went to Harlem to get money from vicks. When we where finished we saw some mopeds sitting in front of a club, we just got on & road. But how did he know?

I said, so.

He said so, so Dinequa they are going to kill you.

I said, Kendu you're bugging.

He said, Dinequa please I don't want you to die. It's cause I broke your heart. Then take it out on me, not on yourself. I don't want to see you in a grave.

I said, "when you broke my heart I want to go to my grave".

He just looked at me. He had this look on his face like he didn't even know how much he really hurt me. I don't think until now that he even knew how much I really loved him. And he looked scared of it. I was like "anyway Kendu the Little Harlem Boys are not coming out here to Queens to kill me".The little Harlem boys they are loyal. But they are not crazy enough to come to Queens. I looked in Kendu eyes and said, Kendu don't worry I'm straight.

When he left I was like oh shit I stole the Little Harlem boys mopeds. Oh shit I stole from them boys and if Kendu knew it was me, oh shit who else. So I gathered the girls and let them know what we did. They where like so let's not go to Harlem again.

I said, peace.

But Angelfire loved Harlem, we used to go to the PAL there.

The PAL recruited Angel from jail. And she, said that she is going there and she didn't give a fuck who knew.

I said, well they are only looking for earths so you're cool.

She said, ok so you don't go there but I will ok.

We were like cool.

One night Angelfire went there and she was cleaning up and someone knocked on the door and she went to answer it. They put a shot gun to the door and blew her head off.

They said, when the cops came her body was at the front door and the rest of her was spattered all over the place.

They said, that there was so much blood that they closed the PAL for a week because it was just so much to deal with. I really miss her. And I knew deep in my heart that I had something to do with it. If only we had walked. If only I didn't start stealing. If only Kendu was here. I really needed him. Damn.

The winter in New York was real cold and Kendu didn't come over as much and everyday I though of him and Angelfire. And when I thought about them I cried. I couldn't even listen to slow music without crying and boy where there a lot of slow songs. WBLS had come on with the "quiet storm" and if you didn't catch that, they had instant replay. What a fucked up and lonely winter it was. But I just kept working and working. And drinking I had a quart of ol'e in the morning and a quart for lunch and a quart to go to bed. That was the only way I could function. I stayed drunk and "blasted". Between the weed and ol'e I was straight. I didn't think about Kendu that much. I guess I didn't. At the job it was cool. I just did billing all day and the people were cool. The World Trade Center was buzzing for Thanksgiving. At that time they needed more installers and I signed up. But the man who ok'd you to become an installer and the head of training said, that I can't install phones with a long skirt on that I needed jeans and a black jacket.

I said it would be no problem I have jeans.

So I got the Lee's together and became a Telephone Installer and then the money really came in, but so did the pills. You install phones so long and the equipment was so heavy. And sometime you where in a four story walk up carrying all that equipment. So a guy that I met there introduced me to "uppers". He said they will keep you awake. I started working all day then signing up for overtime.

I said, oh shit give me one.

And it worked I was up alright and laughing and singing and damn near running up and down the stairs. By Christmas I was an upper person and was no longer drinking o'e. I was drinking Guinness Stout, hot right out of the bottle. My girls chilled also. I mean you couldn't ride mopeds in the New York snow. I turned them on to uppers and they loved it too. Well with everyone high on uppers and drunk the Christmas tree in the lobby of the World Trade Center went down and they blamed the installers. And they where right some good ole boys just got too carried away and tried to climb the tree. Well the World Trade Center was not going to take that, so we had to go to 375 Reed Street. Kendu came up for New Years and told me I love you Dinequa and I will always. He looked at me and seen right in my soul. He said, you're killing yourself. You have "wine o lips". What the fuck is that? I don't know if it was the pills or Guinness but the shit was on. We were like rabbits again, but the feeling never came back and Kendu didn't sing either. It seemed like we were changing. I told him that I had to wear pants at the job because I was an installer. He seemed to not mind as long as when I was with him I wore ¾. He said, please Dinequa, and please stay safe, please! By the time summer came my brother Fuel changed his name to Supreme God and Raif changed his name to The King and Sheila was Shaniqua, but they where really only in name. Supreme and I were some dancing fools. The gods came out with a dance called the six step and damn did we know how to do that. It was like it was part of us. I knew his moves and he knew mine. We use to dance in the park at block parties and everyone used to surround us. Then Supreme use to do this thing where I used to go out of the dance and Shaniqua use to come in. Then we really fucked it up when he use to dance with both of us at the same time.

Dancing helped me forget Angelfire and Kendu. A little. Man music was my life now. And music brought everyone together. I use to work and get paid and go dancing, drank Guinness & take uppers. Either I was dancing in a park with my brother or I was hanging out with Shaniqua in this place called the village at this club called the Garage. Shelia didn't stay Shaniqua for long. And she didn't hang on the block for long, we came together to dance. I think she noticed the change in me too. Hell, everyone noticed. I was mad again. The pain of my lover and Angelfire I must have worn it on my fore head.

At first I couldn't get into the Garage scene, because it use to start at midnight and last until morning. I didn't understand, at first, how Sheila would stay up that long but it was ok. Sheila had clubs and I had my brother. But the more I work the higher I got I was into weed, drinking Guinness & taking uppers and then I picked up cigarettes. I started hanging out with people I worked with. They would go after work to the bars. And I learned how to drink things other than beer. The thing was to order the most expensive thing there was. I like "Courvoisier". It was a smooth drink and it was expensive. After a while the long skirt wouldn't do it at the bars. So I had to take it off. In a way I had to respect Kendu no matter what. But, when I did that was the end of Dinequa Refinement Earth and the beginning of.........

CHAPTER **6**

Rachel

I started hanging out with Italians. They turned me on to the good life. They had lots of money, drugs and their houses where as big as my block. They had pools and man did they eat. And I loved every minute of it. They use to have great parties at their place near Coney Island and I used to bring my girls. With lots of liquor. And lots of weed. I use to come home and show my family all the liquor and my brother and Sheila really liked that. I also started to drink "Pipers". It was a Champaign, the Italians loved their wine, and Champaign. I use to be so drunk that I would wake up on the stoop of my house. And my brothers use to help me in. Even my brothers and sister drank Pipers. Man we used to get drunk all the time. Then I would drive up in cars that used to cost more then my house. And my brothers loved it. One day I was so drunk I went with this guy named Ted my brother's friend. I went over to his house and his mother started breaking. I didn't care what she was saying and believe me when I say I didn't understand a word she was saying. I just left Ted there and went around the corner to Michelle's house. Michelle was a girl who use to tell me to stop drinking and to call Kendu. Michelle was the kind of girl that would give you advice but didn't take it herself. I just needed her when Sheila wasn't there. But, she was no Sheila. So I went over her house and was sitting with her. She was getting ready to go to jail. She showed me what she was bringing a sweater, jacket and long johns.

I asked her why she was going to jail?

She said, prostitution.

I said, I didn't know you was a hoe.

She said she was never good at it that's why she's going to jail.

I said, sure you're right. Well, I said, guess I'll go home and see you when you get out.

She said, ok see you oh yeah call Kendu.

I went to the house and the door was locked. So I knocked on it. My littler brother Raif answered and I said, move. My mother came to the door and said, I'm tired of your shit. I'm tired of the cops coming to my house for you. I want you to leave.

I said, ok just let me get my clothes.

She said, bitch you don't have any clothes here. I couldn't believe it that bitch was throwing me out on the street on a Friday night. Where the fuck do I go.

She said, I don't care.

I went to the corner and my brother Supreme came and said, sis hold up.

I said, what.

He said, where are you going to go.

I said, I don't know. We walked up to the corner of Farmers Blvd and I got on the phone and called the only person I knew to call Kendu. I told him what happened and he said come down here and Sunday I'll bring you back and I'll take care of everything. So I got on the Greyhound and went to Washington. I looked at my brother and sister who ended up on the corner with us. I looked at them and said, bye. It felt funny me leaving them. Then I got on the bus and I was gone. Kendu was happy to see me but I was scared.

I said, I have to go to work Monday what am I going to do.

He said, Dinequa I'll take care of you I love you. You know that don't you?

I said, yes I do. See I knew Kendu loved me but I knew I could never be totally with him again. But, we had a connection. Something stronger than us both. Anyway by that time Kendu had a lot of women. And during those two days that I was there I couldn't answer the phone or go outside. I had to stay inside and not answer the door. And the phone rang a lot and people or women knocked on the door all day. But at night he was mine and he felt good. I told myself that it felt good. But really I didn't, I was now Kendu's quiet little secret.

Sunday Kendu took me back to New York and we went to a house across the street from Dawn Park on the south side. He took me inside and said you can live here and all you have to do is pay the bills ok.

I said, who's house is this?

He said, a friend.

I said, that's dope. I bought a box spring and a mattress but I didn't know how to pay bills so every time the bill would come I had to call Kendu to ask him what to do. And he would tell me. But having your own house was the ultimate dope everyone came over. My brothers use to come over with my little sister, who would come over with her friends and play cards on my floor. They seem to not mind that I didn't have any furniture they just liked being with me. Living in the house was dope and I really stopped paying bills I had to keep everyone high, so Kendu started paying them. Also the house was a hang out where my brothers would come. But then I had other people come over like Sli, a guy I met from the West Side. He was a real tall guy with battle scars all over his face. I called him "scarface". We would drink and smoke lots and lots of weed. I also still had my 5% ways and conversation with the gods like Black a young god who everyone said looked like he could be my brother. Black was so cute and he was so criminal minded. The gods where also changing. Some would be drug heads, some where pimps and then there was Kendu's crew who went to college and wanted to be doctors, lawyers and businessmen. Kendu even had one god who was in this new black magazine as one of the fifty black men to watch. Kendu would pay all the bills but, I knew that it wouldn't last. So when he came over and said, that his parents where selling the house and I had to leave I was not surprised.

Kendu also asked me why am I doing this, acting like this.

I proudly said, the devil made me do it. I still wore my long skirts with my shoes and matching bags. I also had very nice blouses and my pants where silk and I also had some of the best coats anyone every seen. But underneath all that glamour was pain. The pain that I didn't understand. I was so angry and some times my anger was off the charts. I use to get the girls together and just beat up people for no reason. The more the blood the better I felt. The better I felt the more I drank and smoked weed, the more I smoke weed the more I took uppers. I was a walking mess. I use to get so wasted that I didn't even make it in the house. I just slept on the stoop.

Anyway

I moved in Sheila's mother house in a spare room. I paid fifty dollars a week. I had a great time there I started hanging out with Sheila who again was hanging out with Darryl and we partied at the Garage. This place was a gay spot but on Friday's they let straight people party. I never partied at a gay spot but I really never ever knew what a gay person was. I mean this place opened my eyes to so much. I mean the dance had changed no one was doing the six step it was played out. It was all about free style. And speaking of free style so was the dress. Every Friday at midnight we would get dressed, my hair was pink and I wore almost nothing. I never knew how free I started to feel. My clothes was very, um, little to say the least. And the music was great. Man was I opened. I couldn't understand why or how could we stay awake to dance at midnight. Then I found out. We would get out at West 4th Street and buy "purple haze" a tab of acid and wait an hour for it to hit. And when it did I would dance man, acid made you dance and move with no problems. I loved acid and Sheila and I would go to any length to get it. One night we heard about Puerto Ricans in the Bronx that were selling "red barrons" and "snoopy". We were there and it was a little piece of paper with snoopy or the red barron on it. The Puerto Ricans loved us. We were sharp. We used to wear leather pants with matching jackets. And back in the days that was all that. I mean if we had on a pair of pants our jackets and shoes would match. We also had diamonds on our hands. I use to hang with the Italians and they turned me on to diamonds and pearls. I was opened to it. Unlike the Puerto Ricans, I didn't trust them, they just looked like they where up to something. They were fine and all, but they spoke Spanish and I didn't and it seemed like ever time we were there they would speak Spanish. Why when we came around? I don't know but I got the funniest feeling. Standing there high on acid listening to someone speaking another language and I couldn't understand it. Sometimes I was so high that it sounded like I was in a bubble and the Spanish would echo. Loud. If you ever did acid you would know what I mean. The echo sound. But Sheila would go back she loved them. Sheila was so high I think she thought she was Spanish. But not me. I stuck with purple haze.

Sli and Black would come over and I would go with them. But they wouldn't come over together. They didn't even know each other. I dared not to introduce them. I mean Sli was my hood link and Black was my con link.

Sli lived in a house with his mother and sisters & father he was the only son. He asked me not to go to the Garage and lets go see that new Bruce Lee Movie. That was Sli's thing a karate movie. He loved Bruce Lee. I really enjoyed hanging with him. So we went to 42nd St. and I found someone who sold purple haze and you've never seen a karate movie until you've seen it with purple haze. Sly didn't understand my need for acid. But truly I didn't care, he had a need for weed, I guess we were even. At the time I only did weed once in a while. We were good together. Sli was cool and six feet tall he stood really high. When we came out the movies we'd do the new karate moves we learned while watching the movie. We got back on the on the train. Sli would get off at 150th and I got off at 130th. So I got off first. But I notice some guys on the train, I had a bad feeling about that. But Sli said they ain't gonna do shit. But it stuck in me. I really wanted to move off the train. So to make me feel better Sli and I moved to the last car. We were doing our karate moves and it was so cool. By time I got off the train I knew how to do the drunken monkey. And Sli knew how to do the five fingers of death. Yeah we were karate bad asses. As I got off the train I notice those same guys coming closer to us. I looked at Sli I mean it was like it was slow motion. And when the door closed they ran over and stabbed him over and over and over again. I screamed "stop the train!" I grabbed the door to try to open it but, it wouldn't. I looked in Sli's eyes as the life ran out of him. But there was nothing I could do. I ran to the next stop I was out of breath by time I got there. I couldn't get there fast enough. I just knew if I got there I could help. Oh god why did I get off the train. I told him that they were up to no good I just knew it. I got to the next stop there were people all around and cops where all over the place. I pushed through the crowd and with acid everything seemed to be in slow motion. It was like there where hundreds of people all over the place. I finally made it and there he was dead, the smell of his blood was strong. It was all up my noise. I cried and cried a cop grabbed me and said get the fuck out of here.

I said, he's my friend. His name is Sli.

The cop said, I don't give a fuck get out of here.

I couldn't get with it. Like what do you mean.

He said, to this lady cop, hey get her out of here.

I said, to the lady cop "don't you need to know who he is".

They said, we know who he is. He told us his name just before he died. The word died stuck to me like the smell of him, and the look in his eyes. That night I walked all the way to his house and when his mother saw me and didn't see him she knew. I don't know how she knew, but she did.

She cried and said, who are you the ghost of death. I turned around and started walking away. A girl came out and stopped me she said, what happened and I told her. Then we cried together.

The next morning or afternoon I woke up and Sheila's mother said, the phone is for you. It was Black I met up with him at his house in Springfield Gardens he lived with his parents and little brother we called Buster. I sat in the living room and told them what happened last night. His mother sat there hanging on ever word I said. After I told the story his father said, what a shame. He was so young. Then he asked me how do I feel. I said, I was tired.

He said did you have any sleep yet.

I said, a little but every time I would close my eyes I would see his face. It was like his eyes were telling me something. I just wish I could have done something, anything. Just not watch him die. His mother came over to me and said, you poor girl this must be a nightmare for you.

I said, well he's the second friend that I know that got murdered. I mean got killed. Then they looked at me and smiled. From that time on we where like a family. His mother use to come pick me up and take me over their house for supper. I liked them. Black was already like a brother to me. We went every where. The Bronx, Brooklyn I mean every where. And everywhere we went there was the women. All the women that belongs to Black. He kinda reminded me of Kendu. A Mack. He introduces me as his sister. And they ate it up. They used to ask me about him. Meanwhile at the block my girls were becoming unraveled. Nana was becoming more and more withdrawn. She couldn't shake the feeling about Angelfire. She tried to kill herself by cutting her wrist. I couldn't believe it. Then out of no were she's sniffing heroin. She would nod when we tried to talk to her. She just couldn't believe that we stole those bikes and that Angelfire got killed because of it.

I told her that it was not our fault. But, I didn't even believe that, because it was our fault. She was dead because we stole those bikes. But what the fuck Nana stop with the drugs that shit would kill you.

Nana's mother couldn't take it no more she said that she had two other daughters to look after so she moved and took Nana with her. The next time I heard about Nana she had overdosed on a roof top.

The more I came home the more things changed. My brother Supreme and the King where stick up kids. Real life stick up kids. They used to walk right up to peoples cars and stick them up for it. They also was the tallest and most popular on the block fuck that in Queens. Everyone knew my brothers. Even the cops. Which we use to call "see cipher power". The see cipher powers damn near had an office on our block. Looking out for my brothers. They use to come home with all kinds of money, cars and guns. If someone didn't give up the car right away they would get a serious ass whipping.

My little sister was getting drunk She really started drinking like I use to. Every day she was drunk and she was only thirteen. She reminded me of me. I really didn't like to see her like that but what was I going to say. I did it. My father and other brother Craig where closer than ever. He would take Craig all kinds of places and do all kinds of things with him. That would get my other brothers jealous. And when they got jealous they would fight. My father and brother Craig against Supreme and the King. My family was separating and I knew it. But I was too high to do anything about it.

The block was changing too. The kids that lived on it started to grow up. And they where just as bad as we where. The whole block was either like my brothers and I or like my sister and Craig. Either they where car thieves or drug dealers or drunks or just "plain ol' fuck ups".

Then one day I came on the block and a new Family moved in D. with his parents, and sister. D. just came out of jail when I met him. And I thought that was cool running. We had nothing in common. He was a rough neck and thought I was a rough neck too that's about it. I hung with him every chance I could get. I hung with him so much that I stopped paying rent at Sheila's and her mother kicked me out. So I lived with the D. I don't think he could say Dinequa so he called me Butter short for Butterfly. He was the only person that I use to let call me Butter. He had no job and no money. But he always had beer. I use to get off the bus from work and D. was waiting for me with a quart of beer or Guinness.

Through all that, my brother Supreme managed to get a full scholarship to Adelphi University. I couldn't believe it. I was so proud of him. He was so smart but so bad. Bein' smart and bad paid off for him. He became student body president. My brother the King wanted to go to the Marines. My little sister went back to school. And Craig and my brothers made amends.

Maybe I should have stayed away from them but I didn't. Maybe this book would have had a better ending, but I didn't and this book doesn't.

He bought me up there and I was so proud of him. And he knew it. My brother could be president of the United States, I thought to myself. At that college everyone loved him. And when he spoke he used those million dollar words.

One day I got off the bus and everyone was out side.

I said what's up?

They said, your brother the King was shot. I felt the earth move. I walked to the house and my mother let into me.

She said, this is your fault you're the devil's child and you did this. Get out bitch, get out.

I said, my fault I wasn't even here.

She said, that you are like a disease everything you touch dies around you.

I said, is he dead?

She said, the whole families dead thanks to you bitch now get out.

I left and went with D. up to the hospital and there he was my baby brother with a bullet in his back. But he was alive. And he had this look on his face. He looked just like my father. I never noticed that before.

I asked him was he alright?

He said, yeah. Where you been?

I said, at work.

Does it hurt, I asked.

He said, no, not really. Did it hurt when you got shot.

I said, no not really. I smiled at him and he smiled back like it was the first time we ever seen each other. My little brother six feet tall and looking like my father shot. and in the hospital. I felt like I had something to do with this. I know I wasn't there but, I just felt like I had something to do with it. Maybe my mother was right, I am the devil's child. Everything I touch dies. I had to make it right. I didn't know how yet but I had to make it right.

I said, what happened?

He said, nothing sis, just go home. But I couldn't the next day I found out what happened and where. So I went to Murdock where one of the boys lived, I had D. with me. I kicked open the door and said, who shot my brother. They just looked at me in shock.

I said, I will kill your whole family if you don't tell me.

His mother said, damn it, tell her!

They said, some guys came from Brooklyn and started shooting.

I said, some guys from Brooklyn.

He said, yeah they've been coming up here a lot. I don't know why they started shooting they just did. I looked at him and his family and said word is bond.

He said, word is bond.

I said, if I find out that this in not true I will be back. And I won't say anything. You get my drift.

He said, word is bond. I couldn't believe it Brooklyn is it possible that this was the same guys we rob that long time ago. Damn it is my fault.

Everyday after that it was wild, wild west, there were shootings on the block and when the King came out of the hospital he was on crutches.

Then one night the cops came and arrested him. That same night D. was walking down the street and they arrested him too.

They said, my brother and D. shot a cop. I knew they didn't' the whole neighborhood knew they didn't but both got a lot of time for it anyway.

Then my brother Supreme heard about it and came up with the idea if he committed a crime that he would get arrested and go to jail with his little brother. But it didn't work out. I really didn't know how close Supreme & the King were. I guess I really didn't know anything at all about them. Now I had two brothers in jail. I got real drunk and by this time I was putting acid in the beer. I was using so much acid that I didn't even know what was real and what was not. I enjoyed living in this state. I didn't have to know anything because nothing made since.

One day we moved on a quiet block in a big house. The next minute you have two brothers in jail. I really couldn't deal with it. It was just too much to handle. But what could I do. So I continued to go to work and get high. And come back to D. house and on the weekends go visit either him or my brothers. My whole world was visiting someone in jail. Or going to an old friend's grave site. It was something about visiting someone in jail. Everyone you know was there. It looks like my whole Queens was there. At least my brothers and D. were not alone. Did that make any sense? Not Alone.

Then my sister came over D.'s house every time I saw her she looked older. Now at this time it was only her and my mother and brother Craig. My father was away more and more. My brother Supreme had a son who was also living at my mothers house with his mother.

My sister asked me to come to the house. That someone wanted to see me. So I did. I could see in her eyes that she had a sadness. And I knew that I had something to do with it. I thought to myself she must be so lonely. My little sister, watching us all fall apart. But as I got close to the house I could see a limo and I wondered who it was.

It was Kendu. The limo in front of the house was his. He had on a black suit with silk trimming around it. A silk tie with matching shoes. Damn he looked good. I haven't seen him in two years. I sat down near him and said, did you hear about my brothers?

He said, yeah. Then he put his arms around me and I held back the tears of my life and decided not to share them with him. I moved away and said, what.

He looked me in my eyes and said, the most painful thing that you could ever hear. They wanted to be like you when they grew up.

I looked up at him and said, well they are.

He said, are you high?

I said, all the time.

Why?

Why not Kendu what else do I have.

He said, you have me Dinequa you always have me.

I said, what do you want?

He said, you.

I looked in his eyes, those eyes that was my passion and said, really Kendu what do you want?

He said, she's pregnant and my parents want me to marry her.

As he was talking I looked at his hands they where so clean. Then I looked at mine. My nails where chipped and dirty. I closed my hand and continued to listen to him.

I am supposed to marry her today.

I looked at him, what the fuck did you say.

He said, but I will leave her in a minute and marry you.

He said, Dinequa would you marry me.

I said, what?

If you tell me you would marry me I'll marry you today. Then he reach in his pocket and came out with a diamond ring and got on his knees and said, Dinequa would you marry me.

Then Raheem got out of the Limo and looked at me.

I said, Kendu go and get married you don't need me anymore. Everything I touch I destroy, don't let me destroy you.

Raheem came over and said, Kendu we have to go.

I said, peace Raheem.

He said, peach Dinequa. I though you would be the one he marry, I guess I was wrong. Kendu kissed me on the cheek and left. I drank four quarts of beer and smoked a pound of weed to get rid of the pain. I ended up moving to Liberty Ave because the pain was too much on that street. And maybe if I leave I wouldn't bring down my sister & Craig no more.

On Liberty Ave I lived with a girl named Cho-Cho and she was. She also liked to smoke cocaine. I heard of freebase but never did it and I didn't want to do it with her. Everyday I came home from work and there she was basing. One day I came home and she was there with a lot of guys basing as usual and she said, that someone was in the living room waiting for me.

It was Kendu, I haven't seen him in a year. What did he want? He was looking and smelling so good. So I told Kendu that I was basing and if he wanted to try it. Cho-Cho was like what? I said, yeah I base.

I spent my whole check that night. The next morning Kendu said, that school is over and his wife was having a boy.

I said, where is she?

He said, at my mothers.

Then why are you here.

He said, she knows about you.

I told him to leave. That I didn't want him here. Go back to your wife.

He said Dinequa?

I said, yo leave and don't come looking for me again.

So he did.

Me and Cho-Cho based so much in the house over the months the bills stop being paid and once again I had to leave. I got another room off Merrick Blvd. Black use to come over and my little sister too. She would come with her friends and like always they played cards. By this time I was basing everyday, all my money based away. My chest started hurting from doing it too much. But I didn't care. I just wanted to die.

One day Black wanted me to come to his new job in Harlem. So I went. I haven't seen him that much, because I was trying to not cause any more harm. Maybe I shouldn't have gone with him. Maybe, just maybe.

Anyway.

It was off 123rd St. On the first floor. And when I went in I couldn't believe it. When we stepped in there was a table with a lot of girls with no shirts on and just panties. They had base and was putting it into bottles. I looked at Black and he smiled. Man my stomach was jumping up and down. I thought I should have bought my guys and robbed the spot. Black went into the kitchen and started cooking base. There were men around with guns just watching the girls bottling it up.

Black said, what you think.

I said, let's take a hit.

He said, we can't but I'll get some and we can take it back to your apartment.

He told me to sit down and don't touch nothing. I just didn't want to get shot.

Black went upstairs with some guys. It took about an hour. When he finally came back I was sweating. I kept thinking if I grabbed some maybe I'll get away with it. Maybe I'll get one of the guys, but by time I got the nerve Black said, come on let's go.

Man I was so happy to leave. I had to take a shit.

We got in a cab and took it to the corner of my block then we jumped out and ran. The cab driver should have known what would happen. When we got to my apartment I opened the door ran upstairs and sat on the toilet man that felt good.

Black said, how do you spell relief?

I said, S H I T.

I came out and said, what do you do there?

He said, sometimes bagging and sometimes selling.

I said, man I couldn't work there they would kill me for smoking all the product.

Black said, yeah. But I will smoke some with you what would you say. Then he pulled out this brown bag.

Man there must have been fifty of them.

He said, you got a pipe.

I said, know you're right. We smoked so much that I got sick. Black pulled out a foil and said, sniff this.

So I did and man in about ten minutes I was calm and then I ran to the bathroom and threw up.

Black came in and said, sis you're alright.

I tried to lift my head up but it felt heavy.

He said, let me help you to bed.

I laid down.

Black said, sis come meet me tomorrow I'll cook you breakfast.

I said, ok, tomorrow for breakfast. Peace.

Peace.

When I woke up there was a note on my door. Once again I was out. So I went to Sheila's house. She was in Long Island at her fathers, so I had her room. Her mother really liked me and no matter what I did, she always let me back in.

Later that day Linda came down to the house and said, Rachel remember Black.

I said, yeah, ah shit I was suppose to meet him for breakfast. She said, he's dead.

I went right over to his house. His mother said, he was going to the store to get bread to make me French toast and when he came out of the store someone shot & killed him. I just turned around and left.

Moving back to Mangin Ave. my two brothers in jail and my sister was being a big girl. Craig was outside a lot, I guess he had to hold down the fort.

By this time Supreme got married in jail to a girl name Linda who had his son name Supreme. I called him dollar bill.

Living with Sheila's mother was cool although she locked the doors to her room and Sheila's little brothers room when they left, but that was cool cause if she didn't I probably would steal something and sell it for crack.

I started hanging out with a girl name Tiny who lived with her grandparents. And everyone said she looked like Sheila. Well me and Tiny clicked right off. We used to go to 42nd & 10th Ave to rob the prostitutes. Man then we used to take money and smoke base which now they called crack. We were cool together we use to lie like crazy and our lies use to fit together we use to "iron surf". Which is riding on the top of trains. We smoked crack and go iron surfing. She didn't know this but I really wanted to jump off.

Anyway.

Until one day we were with a guy name Buster and he slipped between the train cars and got his legs caught in between the platform and it cut his legs off.

Then we robbed a "number spot" to get money to smoke crack and the next day everyone on the Blvd. were looking for who did it. Someone said, Tiny did. Her grandmother got scared and moved Tiny to Florida. Wouldn't you know it. I heard that the cops where riding by this lot in Florida and noticed a car that had buzzards all around it. They went to check it out. As they got closer, they noticed the windows were fogged up. It was about 90 degrees that afternoon. One of the cops had the bright idea to break the window. And when he did he lost his lunch. The other officer looked inside & called it in. They identified Tiny by her dental records. Whoever killed her left her wallet in the car with her. They said she's been there for at least a week cooking in the hot sun. Dead.

I stayed in Sheila's house and smoked and smoked. My job offered me money to leave and I took it. Hell, I wasn't showing up anymore, anyway. I only went to work to get paid and smoke crack I did this for a long time.

Then one day out of the blue Michael came upstairs to see me and he told me to get dressed and come with him. I did. We went to Hale Avenue to a place where drug dealer played cards and talk shit. We went in and Michael met some of his friends that were already waiting for him.

He said, for me to stay outside and he will be back. So I did. The next thing I knew, I heard shooting and screaming. Then Michael and his friends came running out. Michael jumped in a cab and took off. I was like what the fuck. I walked home thinking why did he bring me. When I got home Sheila's mother said, Michael was looking for me. So I went to his house, he came out and said, that was wild right.

I said, you're crazy.

Then we went to Sheila's house. Michael said, do you have a pipe.

I said, yeah!

He pulled out a lot of crack and we smoked all night long. He left about 6am. I was on the floor looking for that invisible piece that I dropped. I was "fienin" for more. Then the door opened and some one was coming up the stairs. I sat on the bed and waited. It was my brother Supreme and Kendu. Supreme came home and I was happy to see him. I tried to stand up but my legs were weak. And I fell down.

My brother said, see I told you my sister was dead.

Kendu knelled down to me and said, with tears in his eyes. I don't know who you are but you just killed my women. Then he wiped a tear from his eyes and left.

I didn't understand what was their problem. It was a year ago that I seen Kendu so I don't know what's his problem. And why did my brother say I was dead. Then I caught a glance at myself in the mirror.

My hair was nappy and I had dark rings under my eyes. My cheeks were sunk in my face. My face was ashy. My neck looked like a stick was holding up my head. The underwear that I had on was sagging. I looked at my hands my nails were dirty and my thumb had blisters on it.

I smiled and I had 32 teeth and the front two where cracked and there was black stuff on them. And some of my teeth where green. I couldn't believe it. In one year this happened, in one year.

I started thinking about my sister and if she saw me like this, what did she think of me. I now know why I never spent time with Supreme my nephew, wow I wonder what he might have thought about me, my auntie the crack head. Or the drug dealers who I stuck up, they would just say here take it and go. Or Sheila why she keeps going to her fathers and not taking me. She loved me so much she probably couldn't stand to see me like this. And then I thought I'm going to kill myself. I wanted be with my girls Nana, Angelfire, and Tiny. Yeah, that's it. I'll kill myself and then I will die a hero. Like Black and Sli. I looked at the radio that Sheila had and I said, I will push it into some water and electrocute myself. So I went downstairs to the bathroom and filled the tub with water and got in. I bought the phone with me(just incase) I figured that I will look like I was trying to call for help, so that everyone would think it was an accident. I plugged the radio in and turned to BLS and I said, on the next song when it goes off I will kick it in the water and grab the phone. Yeah that's a good plan. But BLS had a lot of commercials on. I looked at my skinny body in the water and said, what happened to you Rachel? What happened to the girl that I knew? The girl with silk under wear. With the matching shoes and bag. The girl that when Kendu saw her his eyes would light up. The girl that my brothers used to say how nice I looked. Then I started to cry. BLS finally played a song:

"Good Morning Heartache" by Ms. Billy Holliday.

As this song played, I must have heard it a million times. But this is the first time I actually listened to it.

It sounded like we shared the same demons.

Is it possible that we had the same pain.

Then I asked myself "out of all the songs in the world that BLS could play, why did they play this song on this day". I didn't ask to be born now look at me. Don't anyone love me. You gave me to a women who hated me from the day I was born. She beat me God. Why? Why was I born on Friday the 13th. Why?, Why? Why? Look at me God, look at me. I'm one of your children you said and look at me. Please God, please. I'm not the devils daughter am I? Please help me. I don't want to die. Please God, help me. They killed my baby! Now they're killing me. Please God Help me. I'm sorry for all that I did. Please Help me God.

"I can't believe this, GOD, after I poured my heart out to you… after I kicked it with you… you had them do an instant replay, play it again, you must want me dead too…I guess you see me like everyone else…a WASTE…"

Then the phone rang it was Joseph. A Puerto Rican boy that I use to mess with a long time ago.

I said, what's up Joseph?

He said, what are you doing?

I said, I'm gonna kill myself.

He said, yeah well don't kill yourself yet meet me on Merrick & Liberty at 7pm ok.

I said, ok.

He said, don't kill yourself ok.

I said, ok!

I hung up the phone and thought I knew there was no God. If he did exist then I knew he wouldn't answer me because, I was the devils child. My mother always said that. She even had a palm reader look at my lines and she said that I was bad luck. My uncle used to say every time he sees me here comes bad luck. You say that enough then I guess it's true.

So I didn't blame God for not answering me. I just wish he did.

I got out the tub and unplugged the radio, went upstairs. I stood there for a while thinking about God, but it made me sad, so I started getting dressed. I put on socks the ones with the holes in it that you had to put in between your toes to keep your toes from sticking out. Then I put on my long johns a pair of sweat pants and my "cords". My beige cords was or use to be real nice, they where the ones with big cords. They use to fit me real nice now they're two pant size too big. Then I put on a tee shirt, a sweat shirt and a "hoody". I thought yeah a hoody just in case I had to run. Then a scarf and a hat.

Then I started walking to Merrick & Liberty to meet Joseph. Joseph was alright, we used to be a couple when I had my room on Merrick, but one day I stole some coke from Mickey who was a big drug dealer on Hall St. Joseph & I went to a motel on Rockaway and we sniffed and fucked.

He said, if you put cocaine on my dick it would stay harder. Yeah it did but it also gave us an infection. And when your nose blows up to the size of a grapefruit and it has puss bumps all over it. Maybe you should stop sniffing coke. I guess his dick almost fell off. Well we just broke up after that.

Then I went downstairs and grabbed my goose down coat if you hit it the feathers would come out.

I started my walk and I thought of Joseph. We use to go dancing all the time at the Limelight. The one in Jersey was our favorite. Our favorite song was "Ain't Nobody" by Chaka Khan. When that music would start you knew it was Chaka. And I use to look at him and he looked at me. Then he use to rub my thighs and the dance was on. I think we could have went on American Bandstand or Soultrain. Until coke, Joseph and I use to look like Fred Astaire and Ginger Rogers. Joseph was a mixture of Spanish and Black and he use to look like he had a tan all the time. We where great on the floor and don't let them play Minnie Riperton

Boy did he love Minnie Riperton. He could dance by himself off her music. But we were better together. Everyone thought we were in love but we were only in love on the dance floor.

Man dancing to a slow jam was not like he was humping all over me. He made you feel sexy holding your hand, his legs between yours and when he use to dip me oh man he was the man on the dance floor.

Thinking of Joseph while I walked made me forget about the bad. It's funny what you think about the day you were going to die. By the time I reached Merrick & Liberty it was dark. I looked behind me down Liberty and it dawned on me that there was no one there. No one at all for a strip that was full of people and cars. There was no one. Alone standing there on this corner so I waited and waited. Then I noticed across the street there where people standing in front of this building. I watched them there where guys and girls gathering in front, and then they went inside. . I thought oh shit that's probably where Joseph would be. Maybe it's a club. Maybe we will get high. Yeah that's it get high.

When I crossed the street I looked inside all I saw was a bunch of people some were standing around and some went into a room. But there was no Joseph. So I stood in front of the building and waited for him. Then a girl came over to me and said, are you going inside.

I said no I'm waiting for someone.

She said, did you check inside.

I said, no.

She said well then she opened the door and said, check.

So I went in. It was warm and everyone was smiling and I thought they were laughing at me. I couldn't leave I don't know why. I went in the room and sat down in the chair close to the door just in case I had to jet.

I looked around and there where seats all over the place, but no Joseph. I don't know but I felt comfortable there. So I relaxed. Then they gave me a blue paper. I looked at it. I didn't understand a word it said.

A girl sat next to me and she was drinking coffee. Then she said, hi I'm Denise what's your name.

I said, my name is Nobody and I looked at her.

She said, welcome Nobody.

Then I looked over and a guy was looking at me. I don't know why, maybe I robbed him or something but it didn't bother me. And shit the way I looked and smelled I would look at me too.

Then the girl sitting next to me said, they are talking to you.

I said, what?

The guy said, who are you?

I said, I'm Nobody and I'm nothing!

It was so quiet that you could hear a pin drop.

Then he said, you have to read.

So I looked at that blue paper and It dawned on me that I didn't go to school to read. I went to play c-lo, and stick teachers in the elevator. But never to read. I mean I didn't have to read 120 lessons, Kendu use to say it so much I memorized it. And no one knew anything. Not even Kendu. Oh, man did I miss him. Oh, did I need him now. And that hit me like a brick to my chest. I looked at the girl and she said, its ok we will help you.

Then I looked over at the guy who was looking at me and he said, it's ok.

I looked back and the girl said, Who. The tears where flowing from my eyes. Damn Rachel you don't even know what the word Who is.

I said, Who.

She said, An

I said, An

She said Addict.

I said, Addict. Then I threw the paper down kicked the chair and said, I'm not an addict. What kind of place is this? I'm out! I walked out and it seemed like everyone came after me.

I said, back the fuck up, I'm not an addict.

They said, that's ok just stay. Please just stay.

I don't know why but I went back to the room and sat down. I mean where else was I going. I didn't hear anything. I thought these people were crazy. I couldn't wait till it was over. I couldn't wait. When It was over they where hugging me and I was like what's up. The last hug I got was from Kendu before he left me to get married. I didn't like being hugged after that.

Then they said, "we're going to get something to eat do you want to come". I didn't have any money and before I told them that.

They said, it's their treat.

It was like they were reading my mind. So we got in this red station wagon. Before we left they said, you have any ID?

I said, yeah why?

They said, you never know when you might be in an accident. Then they laughed.

It was Mike an older guy that owned the station wagon. Then Rob, Denise and a guy named Jerry the same guy that was staring at me. Then we went to White Castle and ordered a bunch of burgers and five hot chocolates.

Then they said, how many you want.

I said, two. When I got my two I swallowed them. I was so hungry, I couldn't remember the last time I ate anything. How did I get like this? I started picking the onions from the bottom of the little box. I was so into getting the last onion that I forgot where I was.

I looked up and Jerry said, do you want some more.

I said, oh no I'm full.

Rob said, well we were hoping that you would want some more because now we had to throw the rest away.

I said, well don't' throw them away I'll eat them. Man they are stupid to even throw these burgers away like that. They are assholes.

Then Mike & Denise came back and said "Rachel", how did they know my name, these people seemed to know a lot about me. Did we do drugs together? Did I rob them? Whatever!

Do you want to get some sleep and something more to eat.

I said, yeah. Well the hospital has a room for you to get some sleep and we would be there tomorrow to see you ok.

I said, ok. Damn when was the last time I slept. I tried not to sleep because when I closed my eyes the dream of my murdered friends would come and haunt me. I didn't care what they said or why they where doing this I was just tired I just had to sleep. I went in the hospital to a place they called detox. It felt like jail. With the shower and the little room. The nurse that was with me was so nice. When I laid down she noticed that I had a twitch and I said, oh that. That's from acid it makes you twitch.

She said oh. How did you get those circles under your eyes?

I said, it's the "zottie bang".

She said what's that?

I said "angel dust".

Man that took me back to the time I had a Vega and we use to go to 123rd and buy zottie bang and Sheila used to make me stop the car on the cross town expressway and search for aliens, while my brothers wife would be in the back seat crying I love you Supreme.

Then the nurse said, are you tired?

I said, yeah. I slept so long that the nurse had to wake me up.

She said, the meeting's starting.

I didn't know what the fuck she was talking about but I said, ok anyway. I just didn't want them to kick me out.

I sat down and there they where Rob, Mike Denise & Jerry just like they said. But my stomach started hurting and I threw up. The nurse took me back to my room and they noticed blood coming out of my rectum. They sent for the doctor. He came took a look at me and sent me to another room. Then he took blood and urine, he made me spit in a cup. Then I laid on my stomach and he took a swab of the blood coming from my rectum.

He said, how long has this been going on.

I said, about a month.

He told the nurse to take something to the lab. Then I laid back on my back he touched my side and said, does that hurt.

I said, yeah.

He said to the nurse she needs an x-ray.

He said your stomach has a lot of scares, is this a bullet hole.

I said, yeah.

He said, when did this happened?

I said, when I was 16.

He said, ok.

Then he pressed down on my right side. I jumped.

He said, does this hurt?

I said, yeah.

Then he took both my arms and said hold them up. But my right one hurts.

Then he touched my right shoulder and told the nurse to add it to the x-ray.

Then he checked my legs and the left one was hurting when he held it up.

He said, that hurts?

I said, yeah. I broke it a long time ago.

He said, nurse add it to the x-ray.

Then I got dressed and went back to the room. The next day I tried to hang myself with my sneaker laces. But they broke. I don't know why I just did. Yeah, I do it's the dreams. I can't take the dreams.

The dreams that I was falling. Or the one I feared most , the black dog.

While I was there, there was a meeting everyday.

And everyday I said, I was nobody and nothing. But I did start to hear them speak. They where telling all these stories about what they done in the streets. I didn't believe a word.

The doctor finally came back and when he did he came with a wheel chair and took me on the elevator and to another part of the hospital and a new bed. They put an IV in my arm and hooked me up to all kinds of machines that beep & beep. Then the doctor came back with two other doctors and a nurse. They told me that my liver is infected and I should be dead. I drank so much beer & liquor that it was killing my insides. Then he said, I have a broken rib and my spine is crooked. The rib came from a fight in the park. They snuck me with a 2 x4. I don't know shit about my spine. That I have a urine track infection & VD. Oh yeah, VD came from selling myself for 2 days to get money for crack & you know I only made $20.00 in two days. That my left fallopian tube were inflamed. That I had a trace of sickle cell and my breathing was abnormal. So they were giving me oxygen, and when they put the tubes in my nose I screamed. It was burning. The doctor took a look and said you have a nasal infection and an ear infection. Then they left.

A nurse came in the room after that and said, how are you still alive. You should be dead.

I said, I tried but it didn't work.

She said, God got you here on time.

I thought God yeah right Joseph did this.

Then the doctor pulled the nurse to the side and she looked at me with tears in her eyes. She put something in my IV and gave me about six pills. Then she sat down next to me.

She said, if you take another drink you will die. Girl you should thank God. He must really love you. You are blessed. Then she started rubbing my arm. Saying that she wanted some of the blessings.

I stayed in the hospital for a long time. They examined me

everyday. And everyday they found something wrong like one day they found a lump under my arm. When I had Sheila's little brother take out my stitches from where, from under my breast the time I got stabbed. It got infected.

The doctor said, he had so much work to do on my body to keep me alive. That he should keep me here another day, just for the rest. He said, I don't know why young lady, but God sure loves you.

He finally let me out the next day with about eight prescriptions. Then he said, hey Rachel be good.

The nurse kept saying God really loves you. You are bless.

How long was I here?

Everyone knew me. The girl with everything wrong. I went outside and there they were, that station wagon, Rob, Denise, Mike & Jerry. I said, thank you for showing up to get me. Look at them.

They said, you can't keep it if you don't give it away. I didn't care what they meant. I was just glad to see them.

I asked, how long was I in the hospital.

They said, you've been in the hospital for a month. We will get your prescriptions filled. And they did. They took me to Sheila's house. And her mother said your mother moved. Where were you? Everyone was looking for you?

I said, in the hospital.

She said, we didn't know what happened to you. She looked scared.

I said, it's cool I'm straight. Then I showed her all the medicine I had to take and went upstairs. I took my medicine. Changed my clothes and went back outside to the station wagon.

They took me around the corner on Farmers to a meeting and they said, hi Rachel and showed me a seat in the front.

They said, this seat is yours. You're in the right place.

I said, yeah. I am. I thought to myself maybe God did hear me after all.

Sometimes I walk by the cool out and I could still see, Tyberius, Babs, Delores, Michael, Sam, Darryl, Eric, Hy-Kim, Mary, Nana, Sandy, Malik, Angelfire, Tiny, Black, Sli, Sheila, Supreme, The King, Craig, Lil' Sis, Kendu & I sitting there drinking a quart of ol' e.

Peace.

CPSIA information can be obtained at www.ICGtesting.com
Printed in the USA

242568LV00002B/62/P